13

ESSENTIAL
CHEMISTRY

ESSENTIAL CHEMISTRY

CARBON CHEMISTRY

ESSENTIAL CHEMISTRY

Atoms, Molecules, and Compounds

Chemical Reactions

Metals

The Periodic Table

States of Matter

Acids and Bases

Biochemistry

Carbon Chemistry

Chemical Bonds

Earth Chemistry

ESSENTIAL CHEMISTRY

CARBON CHEMISTRY

KRISTA WEST

CHELSEA HOUSE
PUBLISHERS
An imprint of Infobase Publishing

CARBON CHEMISTRY

Chelsea House
An imprint of Infobase Publishing
132 West 31st Street
New York NY 10001

Library of Congress Cataloging-in-Publication Data

West, Krista.
  Carbon chemistry / Krista West.
    p. cm. — (Essential chemistry)
  Includes bibliographical references and index.
  ISBN 978-0-7910-9708-3 (hardcover)
  1. Carbon. 2. Carbon—Composition. I. Title.

  QD181.C1W47 2008
  546'.681—dc22   2007051318

Chelsea House books are available at special discounts when purchased in bulk quantities for businesses, associations, institutions, or sales promotions. Please call our Special Sales Department in New York at (212) 967-8800 or (800) 322-8755.

You can find Chelsea House on the World Wide Web at http://www.chelseahouse.com

Text design by Erik Lindstrom
Cover design by Ben Peterson
Composition by North Market Street Graphics
Cover printed by Bang Printing, Brainerd, MN
Book printed and bound by Bang Printing, Brainerd, MN
Date printed: January, 2010
Printed in the United States of America

10 9 8 7 6 5 4 3

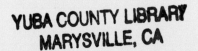

CONTENTS

1   **Introduction to Carbon Chemistry**   1

2   **A Brief Review of Atoms and Elements**   7

3   **Carbon Compound Chemistry**   16

4   **Biomolecules**   35

5   **The Carbon Cycle**   42

6   **The Atmosphere and Climate**   59

7   **Global Warming**   67

8   **Carbon and Energy**   75

9   **Carbon Products**   84

Periodic Table of the Elements   92

Electron Configurations   94

Table of Atomic Masses   96

Glossary   98

Bibliography   105

Further Reading   107

Photo Credits   110

Index   111

About the Author   117

Introduction to
Carbon Chemistry

Carbon is something we encounter every day. Graphite, which is pure carbon, is the "lead" in pencils. Diamonds are carbon and so is charcoal. Some hard coals are up to 98% carbon. Carbon is also present in all living things. Forests, for example, are made almost entirely of carbon-containing compounds. Carbon and carbon compounds are widely used as raw materials in industrial products. Many plastics, detergents, foods, and medicines are made from carbon-containing compounds.

The oil, coal, and natural gas we burn for energy are made up mostly of carbon. Our dependence on these **fuels** has, in recent years, caused economic problems, but even more importantly, it has contributed to the worldwide problem of global warming. Most scientists now believe that the burning of carbon-based fuels has increased the concentration of carbon dioxide in the **atmosphere**, and that this, in turn, has resulted in rising

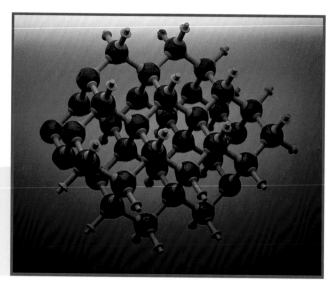

Figure 1.1 A diamond is made up entirely of carbon atoms arranged in crystal form.

temperatures at Earth's surface. Evidence for global warming is visible in the unprecedented melting of Arctic and Antarctic ice and in the gradual retreat and disappearance of glaciers in many parts of the world.

Carbon chemistry, or **organic chemistry**, was originally the study of compounds obtained from living things. It was believed that only living things had the vital force required to synthesize these chemicals. In contrast, **inorganic chemistry** was the study of rocks and minerals and various gases and the compounds obtained from them. The distinction between organic and inorganic chemistry was proved inaccurate in 1828, when the German chemist Friedrich Wöhler synthesized urea in his laboratory. Previously, this substance had been obtained only from living things. It is now known that a substance made by a living thing and the same substance made in a laboratory are, indeed, identical.

HISTORY OF CARBON USE

The earliest use of carbon fuels began with the ancestors of modern humans, who were the first to harness the power of fire, possibly as far back as 800,000 years ago. This makes fire one of the first technologies used by humans. The ability to cook food, for example,

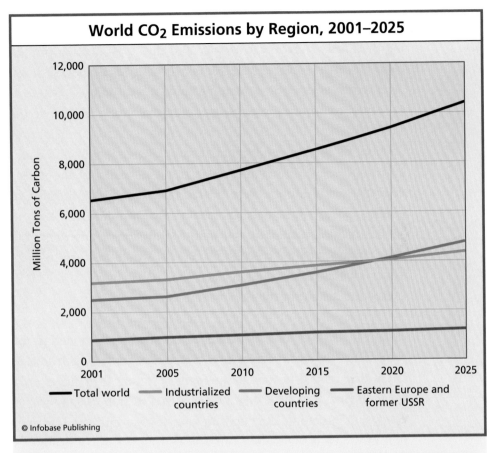

Figure 1.2   It is estimated that global emission of carbon dioxide will continue to rise well into 2025.

meant humans could expand the range of foods that were safe to eat. The advantages of cooked food had probably been recognized already from the "cooked" remains of plants and animals killed in wildfires. In addition to its use in cooking, fire provided heat and light and protection from wild animals.

Charcoal, Coal, and Coke

Humans have been making and using charcoal for about 6,000 years. Charcoal is made by heating wood in the absence of oxygen (air). The use of charcoal in metallurgy was a necessary technology for making bronze and iron during the Bronze and Iron Ages. During the Bronze Age, charcoal was used in the production of pure copper, which could then be combined with tin to make bronze. Steel is made from iron containing about 2% carbon.

Small coal mines were in operation in Europe as early as the 1200s. By the 1700s, charcoal was in great demand for metal production. By the mid-1700s, humans were dependent on wood and coal to power steam engines. As a result, so many of the forests in England and Europe were cleared that there was a shortage of lumber. Coke, a fuel made by heating coal, produces little or no smoke, making it more useful than coal in conditions where the large amount of smoke produced by coal would be harmful. The discovery that coke could replace charcoal in metal production caused the decline of the charcoal industry.

The invention of the steam engine is a prime example of a carbon-fueled machine that changed the world. Developed in the early 1700s, the steam engine used fire to heat water, which created steam that moved pistons in an engine. Among their many uses, steam engines pumped water and powered steamboats and trains. The steam engine was the driving force for the Industrial Revolution of the early eighteenth century. During this time, the use of carbon-based fuels, mainly coal, skyrocketed.

Coal is widely used today in power plants around the world, particularly in India and China, which are the most heavily populated countries in the world. The coal-powered plants cause enormous air pollution. Pollutants from a coal-burning Chinese power plant have been found in the mountains of California, proving that the effects of burning coal are felt not only locally but also worldwide.

Oil

Although oil wells were dug by the ancient Chinese as early as the fourth century, most oil used before the mid-1800s came from puddles that seeped onto Earth's surface. This oil was used as a fuel for lamps and in medications and building materials. In the

TABLE 1.1 A BRIEF HISTORY OF CARBON AND HUMANS

DATE	SIGNIFICANCE
Prehistory	Cavemen learn to make and use fire (approximately 800,000 years ago).
3750 BC	Earliest known use of carbon is by the Egyptians. Charcoal was used to make bronze and as a smokeless fuel for home fires.
1500 BC	Egyptians use charcoal to absorb smells from healing wounds.
450 BC	Phoenicians use charcoal to store and preserve drinking water; Hindus use charcoal to filter drinking water.
157	Romans record over 500 medical treatments using carbon.
1200s	Small coal mines come into operation in Europe.
1500s	Europeans explore the world, looking primarily for new carbon resources (food, fur, wood, etc.).
1700s	Widespread use of carbon (fossil fuels) for energy begins in Europe with the Industrial Revolution and the invention of the steam engine.
1785	First formal recognition of charcoal's ability to absorb smells and colors.
1812	British chemist Sir Humphry Davy identifies coal and diamonds as being made of the element carbon.
1854	London uses charcoal filters to remove smells and gases from city sewers.
1869	Russian chemist Dmitri Mendeleyev places carbon in the periodic table.
1882	The first coal-powered electricity plant is constructed in the United States to supply the city of New York.
1901	Commercial development of activated charcoal begins; used in filters and filtration processes.
1940s	The petrochemical industry (makers of carbon-based synthetic materials such as plastics) begins to flourish.
1950s	Some consumers begin to switch from burning coal to natural gas to make energy.
2000s	Global warming, caused by excess carbon dioxide and other greenhouse gases in the atmosphere, becomes a major, international political issue.
2002	5,000 million tons of coal are produced worldwide; the coal is used mostly for the generation of electricity.

Note: This timeline is not intended to be a complete history of humans and carbon; instead, it is a brief sampling of some major events in carbon/human history.

mid-1800s, kerosene obtained from the distillation of oil replaced other fuels, particularly whale oil, in lighting devices.

The dependence on oil, which is behind many current economic and climate problems, did not begin until the invention of the internal combustion engine and automobiles. In 1900, 4,192 automobiles were built. By 1968, there were 271 million cars, trucks, and buses worldwide. In 1985, the number of these vehicles had jumped to more than 484 million, and by 1996, it had reached 671 million. The number of vehicles on the roads is increasing rapidly as developing countries, particularly India and China, become wealthier. Both countries already suffer serious air pollution caused by the carbon emissions from cars and trucks, as well as the burning of coal.

Natural Gas

The use of natural gas for lighting streets began in the 1820s. Its use for lighting in homes in New York and other cities did not occur until the latter part of the 1800s. That use ended with the invention of the light bulb and the widespread installation of electrical service. Today, natural gas is used to heat homes, to produce electricity, and as an industrial fuel.

A Brief
Review of Atoms
and Elements

This chapter provides some basic information on the nature of atoms and elements, which will help to clarify the discussion of carbon chemistry that follows.

ATOMS

All matter is made up of **atoms**, tiny particles consisting of a positively charged central **nucleus** surrounded by a cloud of negatively charged particles.

The nucleus of an atom contains two types of particles. There are positively charged particles called **protons** and electrically neutral particles called **neutrons**. In the space around the dense nucleus of an atom are negatively charged particles called **electrons**. The amount of positive charge on a proton is equal to the amount of negative charge on an electron. The number of electrons in the space around the nucleus is equal to the number of protons in the nucleus so that the atom as a whole is electrically neutral. The number of protons in the nucleus determines what kind of atom it is—for example, carbon, hydrogen, or oxygen. The distribution of the electrons around the nucleus determines the chemical properties of the atom.

In the course of chemical reactions, an atom may gain or lose electrons. When this happens, the atom is no longer electrically neutral—it has a negative or positive electrical charge. A particle of this kind is called an **ion**.

ROBERT BOYLE

The English chemist and physicist Robert Boyle (1627–1691) first suggested the modern definition of an element. Before Boyle, chemists were on a different track entirely. The ancient Greeks were actually the first to suggest that all things on Earth were made of the elements. But the Greeks believed there were only four basic elements: earth, air, fire, and water. Some early chemists believed that they could change one "element" (usually a common and cheap metal) into another "element" (usually gold). Not surprisingly, none of these experiments worked.

It was not until the mid-1600s that chemists began to reject the idea of the Greeks' four basic elements. In 1661, Boyle suggested the definition of "element" as we know it—something that cannot be reduced to a simpler substance by normal chemical means—and suggested there were many more than four elements. He is considered the founder of the modern element and one of the first true chemists.

ELEMENTS AND ISOTOPES

At present, there are 117 known kinds of atoms, each with a characteristic number of protons in the nucleus. Each kind of atom is a different **element**, thus there are 117 known elements. Of these, 92 occur in nature. The rest have been created only in laboratories. The number of protons in an atom determines which element it is. For example, all atoms of carbon contain six protons, and all atoms that contain six protons are carbon atoms. All hydrogen atoms have one proton.

All elements are assigned a one- or two-letter **chemical symbol**, which is used in writing out **chemical formulas** and reactions. The names and symbols for some of the elements commonly found in living things are: carbon, C; oxygen, O; hydrogen, H; nitrogen, N; phosphorus, P; and sulfur, S.

There can be varying numbers of neutrons in the atoms of an element. Most carbon atoms have six neutrons, but there are also carbon atoms with seven and eight neutrons. The differing numbers of neutrons does not affect the chemical properties of the atom. The different forms of an element that vary only in the number of neutrons in the atoms are called **isotopes**. Isotopes are named according to the total number of protons and neutrons they contain. Thus the isotopes of carbon with six, seven, and eight neutrons are called carbon-12, carbon-13, and carbon-14, respectively. Hydrogen has isotopes with one, two, and three neutrons. The most common form of hydrogen has only one neutron.

ATOMIC NUMBER AND ATOMIC MASS

The number of protons in an atom is called its **atomic number**. Thus, the atomic number identifies the element. For example, the element with an atomic number of six is carbon.

The total number of protons plus neutrons in an atomic nucleus determines its **atomic mass**, which is often called **atomic weight**. For example, the mass of an atom that contains six protons and

CARBON DATING

Scientists commonly use the isotope carbon-14 as a tool to determine the age of objects composed of material that was once alive. Determining the age of something using carbon isotopes is called carbon dating, or radiocarbon dating.

The isotope used in carbon dating is carbon-14, which is radioactive. The nuclei of radioactive atoms undergo a breakdown process called decay, in which they emit energy and, sometimes, particles. The result of radioactive decay is that the atom changes into a more stable isotope of a different element. Carbon-14, for example, decays to form nitrogen-14, a stable isotope.

The half-life of carbon-14 is 5,730 years. This means that in a given sample of carbon-14, half the atoms will decay in 5,730 years. During the next 5,730 years, half the remaining atoms will decay. This continues until there are no carbon-14 atoms left.

Most of the carbon on Earth exists as C-12 and C-13 isotopes because these forms are stable, meaning they are not radioactive. Carbon-14 is produced in the upper atmosphere by radiation from the Sun. Plants take in carbon in the form of carbon dioxide during photosynthesis, the process that uses carbon and energy from sunlight for the synthesis of carbohydrates. Animals take in the carbon when they eat plant matter. In living organisms, the relative amount of carbon-14 remains constant—some is taken in and some decays. When an organism dies, it stops taking in new carbon. Over time, the amounts of C-12 and C-13 contained in the dead organism remain the same because they are both stable isotopes. But the amount of C-14 decreases over time as the isotope decays predictably into its new form. Scientists can measure the amounts of stable carbon isotopes and compare the results to the amount of C-14. The more the C-14 has decayed, the older the remains being tested.

Because all living things take in carbon, the age of their remains and products made from living things can be determined by using carbon dating. The age of buried seashells, cotton fibers in clothing, wood, and bone can all be determined with carbon dating. The technique can be used for materials up to about 60,000 years old. At that point, most of the carbon-14 atoms have decayed, thus, no meaningful comparison can be made.

Figure 2.1   This shows model Kennewick Man, who was estimated to be at least 9,000 years old through the use of carbon dating.

Carbon dating is a common and useful tool in science. The age of the Kennewick Man, for example, was determined by using carbon dating. Kennewick Man is the name given to the remains of a male skeleton found in Washington State in 1996. Through studying the carbon isotopes contained in the bones of the ancient body, the National Park Service determined that Kennewick Man was at least 9,000 years old and officially of Native American origin.

six neutrons is twelve. The atomic mass of the isotope carbon-12, which has six protons and six neutrons, is twelve.

COMPOUNDS AND MOLECULES

The atoms of various elements can combine to form new substances. For example, atoms of the elements hydrogen and oxygen combine to form water. This chemical combination of atoms of two elements to form a new product is an example of a chemical reaction. Note that the properties of water, a colorless, tasteless liquid, are very different from those of its constituent elements, which are both gases. A substance, such as water, made from the chemical combination of atoms of two or more elements is called a **compound**. While an element cannot be broken down into a simpler form by normal chemical means, a compound can be broken down into atoms of

ALCHEMY

For more than 2,000 years beginning in the Middle East and Far East, "natural philosophers" practiced alchemy, which involved the study of a combination of science and nature, art, and various spiritual and philosophical ideas. Practitioners of alchemy were known as alchemists, and they were best known for their belief that base metals, such as lead, copper, and tin, could be turned into gold. Although they never succeeded in this quest, they are now thought to have made some real advances in the science of chemistry. Because they were constantly experimenting with different techniques and chemicals, they discovered some useful chemical processes, such as testing ores and the production of ceramics, paints, and dyes. Perhaps more importantly, they also showed that actually doing experiments was crucial to the advancement of knowledge.

its constituent elements. A **molecule** is the smallest unit of a compound; its constituents are the same as those in the compound and are present in the same proportions. A water molecule consists of one oxygen atom bonded to two hydrogen atoms; therefore, its formula is H_2O.

THE PERIODIC TABLE

Many elements, including carbon, had been discovered by the mid-1800s, and chemists were looking for a way to organize the information that had been discovered. In 1869, the Russian chemist Dmitri Mendeleyev (1834–1907) created the first accurate **periodic table**, an organized chart of all the elements and their distinguishing characteristics. The periodic table, which has been revised and expanded since Mendeleyev, is still one of the most useful tools in chemistry.

In his table, Mendeleyev arranged the elements according to atomic mass, leaving spaces for the elements that were not yet known. Carbon was placed in the sixth position. The modern periodic table is organized differently. While today we know that Mendeleyev made a few mistakes, carbon still remains in the sixth position.

In the periodic table, the elements are arranged vertically into groups and horizontally into rows, or periods. Mendeleyev's table had eight groups, but the modern periodic table has eighteen. In both Mendeleyev's and the modern periodic tables, the vertical groups show elements with similar properties. In the modern periodic table, carbon is in group 14, along with silicon, tin, and lead. Mendeleyev's groups were based on the characteristics of the elements. Later developments showed that these recurrent characteristics depend on the arrangement of the atoms' electrons. The horizontal rows show elements in order of increasing atomic number, left to right.

The elements in a group share certain properties. Thus, in making his periodic table, Mendeleyev had to decide when to continue

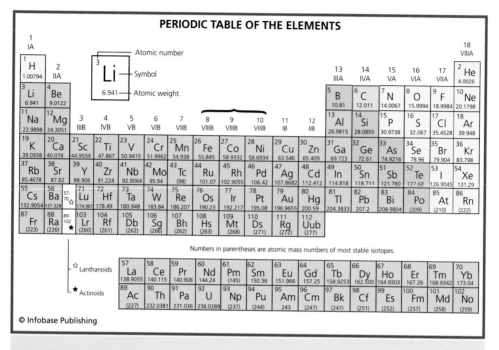

Figure 2.2   This is the periodic table—note the placement of carbon in group 14 and period (horizontal row) 2.

placing the elements in a period (in the horizontal row) according to atomic weight and when to start a new period and place them in a particular group (in a vertical row). For example, he placed potassium (K) under sodium (Na) in group 1 instead of placing it near chlorine in group 8. He did this because sodium and potassium share a number of characteristics: Sodium and potassium are both solids that have low densities and low melting points; they both react with water to give off hydrogen gas; and they both are good conductors of electricity. Chlorine, on the other hand, is a gas and is a poor conductor of heat and electricity.

A study of the atoms in the groups and periods reveals a trend in the size of atoms moving from top to bottom and left to right of the periodic table:

- The more electron shells in an atom, the larger the atom, thus the size of the atoms increases from top to bottom through a group in the periodic table.
- Generally, the size of the atoms decreases from left to right across a period of the periodic table.

Another interesting fact about the size of atoms is that atoms that have lost an electron are smaller than the original atom, while atoms that have gained an electron are larger than the original atom.

Carbon Compound Chemistry

Carbon is an interesting element and is exceedingly important to all living things on Earth. It forms the backbone of all kinds of structural and functional compounds necessary for life, including DNA, proteins, fats, and carbohydrates. It is interesting chemically because of its amazing ability to form compounds, bonding not only with atoms of other elements, but also with other carbon atoms.

THE CREATION OF CARBON

The creation of carbon, like that of the other elements, is part of the history of the universe. All but the lightest of the natural elements were created in the cores of stars at extreme temperatures. In this process, called nucleosynthesis, protons are smashed together to form nuclei with more and more protons (heavier and heavier elements). Carbon was formed by collisions of three helium nuclei, each

Figure 3.1 In a star, protons collide to form heavier and heavier elements in a process called nucleosynthesis.

of which contained two protons. When the carbon-containing stars died, the resulting explosions dispersed the elements, including carbon, throughout the universe. It is thought that billions of years ago, the Solar System solidified out of a cloud of material left from these dead stars, forming the Sun and planets that now contain these elements. In addition, meteorites and other carbon-containing objects bombarded the surface of Earth, incorporating even more carbon into Earth's composition. Carbon is the fourth most abundant element in the universe after hydrogen, helium, and oxygen.

FORMS OF CARBON

Some elements have several different forms. In the case of carbon, charcoal was the only recognized form until early in the nineteenth century. The name "carbon" actually comes from the Latin word *carbo*, meaning charcoal. In 1812, Sir Humphry Davy used sunlight to set a diamond on fire. This demonstration, combined with his scientific explanation, proved that diamonds were made of pure carbon. Around the same time, Davy also showed that coal was another form of carbon. Graphite, which is the lead in pencils, is

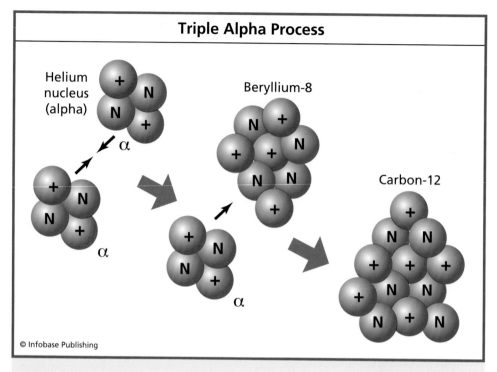

Triple Alpha Process

Helium nucleus (alpha)

Beryllium-8

Carbon-12

Figure 3.2 **In the triple alpha process, three helium nuclei collide to eventually produce carbon. This process occurs in extremely hot stars.**

still another form of carbon. These different forms of an element are called **allotropes**.

Although humans have used, recognized, and studied carbon for centuries, modern scientists are still learning new things about this element. In 1985, a group of researchers at Rice University in Houston, Texas, discovered still another form of carbon, which was named **fullerene**. Fullerene consists of multiple carbon atoms joined together in spherical or tubelike shapes. Fullerenes are discussed in more detail in Chapter 9.

PHYSICAL PROPERTIES OF CARBON

The **physical properties** of a substance are those attributes that can be observed without any chemical changes. Examples of physical

TABLE 3.1 SOME BASIC PROPERTIES OF CARBON

PROPERTY	DEFINITION	CARBON (C)
Chemical series	A group of elements that has certain properties in common	Nonmetal
Appearance	What the element looks and feels like at normal room temperature	Black (graphite) Colorless (diamond)
Hardness	Measured on a scale of 1 to 10, with 10 being the hardest	1–2 (graphite) 10 (diamond)
Atomic number	The number of protons in the nucleus	6
Atomic weight	The total number of protons and neutrons in the nucleus	12 (carbon-12 isotope)
Melting point	The temperature at which a solid changes into a liquid	6,332°F (3,500°C) (graphite)
Boiling point	The temperature at which a liquid changes into a gas	8,726°F (4,830°C) (graphite)

properties are color, physical state (solid, liquid, or gas), hardness, luster, ability to conduct heat and electricity, and density.

Carbon is a solid and one of the eighteen nonmetallic elements. The **nonmetals** have a number of common properties:

- They are poor conductors of electricity.
- They have a dull surface.
- They are brittle.
- They vary greatly in their melting and boiling points.

The different allotropes of carbon have very different physical properties. Graphite (used as pencil lead) is black and soft, while diamonds are clear and very hard. On a scale of 1 to 10, graphite has a hardness of between 1 and 2, while diamonds have a hardness of 10.

Figure 3.3 Graphite makes up the lead in pencils.

CHEMICAL PROPERTIES OF CARBON

The **chemical properties** of a substance depend on whether the substance can undergo a particular chemical reaction and under what conditions it can react. The way that an atom or molecule reacts depends on the number and arrangement of its electrons.

Carbon has six electrons. These electrons reside in two "shells" that surround the nucleus. In all atoms, the innermost shell can contain only two electrons when filled. The innermost shell of the carbon atom contains two electrons. In carbon, the second shell, which is farther from the nucleus, contains four electrons. This shell can contain up to eight electrons. The number and organization of electrons in the outermost electron shell is critical to how an atom behaves with other atoms. Atoms are most stable when the outermost electron layer is full, which means that it contains the maximum number of electrons. For a carbon atom to attain its most stable configuration, it must have eight electrons in its outer electron shell.

Because the outermost shell of a carbon atom contains only four electrons, these atoms can gain stability by losing four electrons, adding four electrons, or sharing four additional electrons from another atom. When an atom loses electrons to another atom, adds electrons from another atom, or shares electrons with another atom, a **chemical bond** is formed. A chemical bond acts to hold atoms together. The strengths of the bonds vary, depending

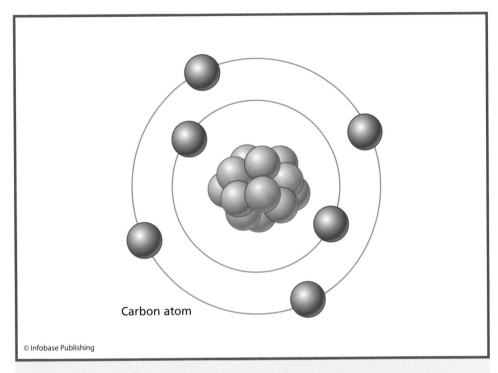

Carbon atom

Figure 3.4   A carbon atom has six electrons that occupy two electron shells.

on what type of bond it is and which atoms are involved, because the atoms of different elements have different chemical properties. Carbon atoms form chemical bonds with other carbon atoms as well as with atoms of other elements.

Types of Bonds

Carbon can form three different kinds of bonds that involve the sharing of electrons. These are called single, double, and triple bonds, depending on how many pairs of electrons are being shared with another atom. This can be another carbon atom, or it can be an atom of another element.

In a **single bond**, two atoms share one pair of electrons. In this electron pair, both electrons can come from one atom or each atom can donate an electron. In a **double bond**, two atoms share two

MEMORIAL DIAMONDS

So-called "memorial" diamonds are a recent trend in the jewelry industry. They are diamonds made—quite literally—from human remains. A number of companies now offer to cremate the body of a loved one or pet and use the carbon contained in the body to create a diamond gemstone. The new diamonds, forms of pure carbon, are marketed as the ultimate, wearable keepsake of the dearly departed.

Traditionally, synthetic diamonds are made from graphite. Since the 1950s, scientists have known how to use pressure and heat to manufacture synthetic diamonds. Gradually, the quality of the synthetic gems has improved. Today, it is difficult to tell a good synthetic diamond from a natural stone. According to the American Museum of Natural History, currently about 80 tons of synthetic diamonds are manufactured each year.

There are currently few statistics on the popularity of memorial diamond creations, but leading manufacturers stress the ease and accessibility of the process as if it is quite common. Further, they push the latest trend: creating diamonds from the carbon contained in still-living people. With a lock of hair and a few thousands dollars, anyone can turn themselves into a gemstone.

pairs of electrons. In a **triple bond**, two atoms share three pairs of electrons.

In large organic, or carbon-based, compounds, there are often long chains of carbon atoms, which can be straight-chain or branched. Hydrogen and oxygen are the atoms that are most commonly attached to the carbons, but the atoms of various other elements are often included.

CARBON COMPOUNDS

Common examples of carbon compounds include carbon dioxide (CO_2, exhaled when we breathe), table sugar ($C_{12}H_{22}O_{12}$), chalk ($CaCO_3$), and natural gas (mostly CH_4). Because there are so many different carbon compounds in nature, it is impossible to learn the name of each one. Instead, groups of carbon compounds are named according to their chemical makeup and structural characteristics.

Naming Carbon Compounds

The name of a carbon compound shows how many carbon atoms it contains, the type(s) of chemical bonds present between the carbon atoms, and the other atoms bonded to the carbon chain. The word "methane," for example, shows that the compound has one carbon atom with only single bonds. All carbon compounds with one carbon atom begin with the prefix "meth." In this case, the "-ane" ending shows that the compound contains only single bonds. All carbon compound names follow these rules.

The second part of the name designates the types of bonds present: The ending "-ane" designates single bonds; the ending "-ene" designates double bonds; and the ending "-yne" designates triple bonds. In addition to the different endings, there is a convention for numbering the carbon atoms in a compound. When there is more than one type of bond in a compound, the location of each bond type is shown by including the number of the specific carbon atom where the bond is located. These naming conventions allow chemists to communicate accurately with other chemists when dealing with unfamiliar carbon compounds. As a simple example, consider an unknown substance called "ethene." From the rules stated above, it should be clear that this compound has two carbon atoms (because it begins with "eth-") and that the carbons are joined by a double chemical bond (because it ends in "-ene"). The common name for ethene is "ethylene."

The number of carbon atoms and the type of bond that form the name of a carbon compound is shown using the prefixes and suffixes in Table 3.2.

TABLE 3.2 NAMING CARBON COMPOUNDS

FIRST HALF OF THE NAME	NUMBER OF C ATOMS	EXAMPLES
meth-	1	Methane (CH_4), principal component of natural gas
eth-	2	Ethane (C_2H_6), component of natural gas
prop-	3	Propane (C_3H_8), common fuel for gas grills
but-	4	Butane (C_4H_{10}), used as a fuel
pent-	5	Pentane (C_5H_{12}), used as a fuel and a solvent
hex-	6	Hexane (C_6H_{14}), constituent of gasoline
hept-	7	Heptane (C_7H_{16}), constituent of gasoline
oct-	8	Octane (C_8H_{18}), constituent of gasoline
non-	9	Nonane (C_9H_{20}), used in kerosene, jet fuel, diesel fuel
dec-	10	Decane ($C_{10}H_{22}$), used in kerosene, jet fuel, diesel fuel
SECOND HALF OF THE NAME	**TYPE OF BOND**	**EXAMPLES**
-ane	Single	Methane (CH_4), principal component of natural gas
-ene	Double	Ethene (C_2H_4), ripens fruit and opens flowers
-yne	Triple	Ethyne (C_2H_2), or acetylene, fuel used in welding torches

HYDROCARBONS

A **hydrocarbon** is a compound that consists only of carbon and hydrogen atoms. Each contains a skeleton of carbon atoms bonded to varying numbers of hydrogen atoms. Hydrocarbons include alkanes, alkenes, alkynes, and aromatic hydrocarbons.

Alkanes

Hydrocarbons with only single bonds are called **alkanes**, and all of their names end with "–ane." Methane (CH_4), the simplest alkane, consists of one carbon atom bonded to four hydrogen atoms. Each of the four hydrogen atoms has one electron. These electrons pair with carbon's four outer electrons to create four single bonds.

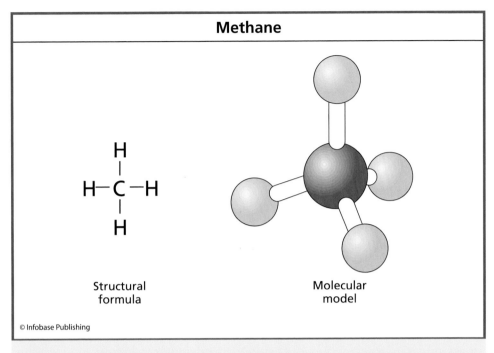

Methane

Structural
formula

Molecular
model

Figure 3.5   Chemists use the structural formula to show a visual layout of the elements and bonds present in a compound. The molecular model shown here provides a three-dimensional view of the arrangement of atoms in a compound as expressed by the compound's chemical formula. For example, the molecular formula of the methane molecule above illustrates the chemical formula CH$_4$.

Most alkanes are obtained from the separation of crude oil into various fractions, depending on their boiling points. The first four alkanes are gases. Methane is the main component of natural gas. Propane and butane are also used as fuels. Propane is used for home heating, stoves, and clothes dryers and as a fuel in specially adapted vehicles. The next four alkanes—pentane through octane—are liquids. Various forms of these alkanes are the main constituents of gasoline. Alkanes from nonane (9 carbons) to the 16-carbon hexadecane are used in kerosene and in diesel and jet fuel.

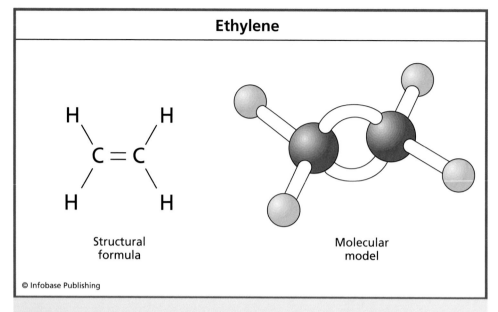

Ethylene

Structural formula

Molecular model

© Infobase Publishing

Figure 3.6   The chemical formula for ethylene can be written as C_2H_4.

Alkanes are often found in natural systems. They are the main constituents in the atmospheres of the planets Jupiter, Saturn, Uranus, and Neptune. Methane is also thought to have been a major component of the atmosphere of the early Earth. Natural gas and oil are primarily made of alkanes.

Alkenes

Hydrocarbons with one or more carbon-to-carbon double bonds are called **alkenes**. The names of alkenes end with "-ene." Ethene, or ethylene, the simplest alkene, has two carbon atoms connected by a double bond. The double bond consists of two pairs of shared electrons, one pair from one carbon atom and one pair from the other carbon atom. Each of the carbons also has two single bonds with hydrogen atoms so that the formula for the compound can be written as C_2H_4.

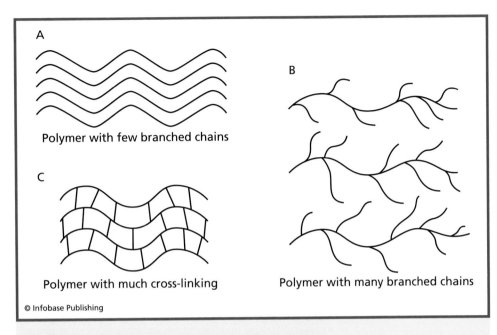

A

Polymer with few branched chains

B

C

Polymer with much cross-linking

Polymer with many branched chains

© Infobase Publishing

Figure 3.7 Above are three kinds of polymer chains.

Ethylene is the most widely used organic industrial compound. It is used in the manufacture of polyethylene, which is the most widely used plastic in the world. It is found, for example, in plastic grocery bags and in milk bottles. In addition to plastics, ethylene is used in the synthesis of many different organic chemicals, including ethylene glycol, which is used as antifreeze in cars and trucks. Ethylene is also found in living things. It is a plant hormone that stimulates the ripening of fruit. Vegetables such as tomatoes are sometimes picked when they are still green and then, at the last minute, treated with ethylene to hasten ripening when they are about to be sold.

The three-carbon alkene, propylene, is also an important industrial compound. It is used in the production of the plastic polypropylene, which is used in molded parts, electrical insulation, and packaging. Propylene is also used in the production of a wide variety of chemicals.

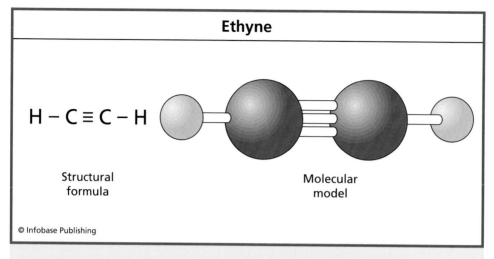

Ethyne

$$H - C \equiv C - H$$

Structural
formula

Molecular
model

© Infobase Publishing

Figure 3.8   The chemical formula for ethyne can be written as C_2H_2.

Polyethylene and polypropylene are both **polymers**, chemicals that consist of long chains of small repeating parts, or units. The Greek word for "parts" is *meros*, and *poly* means "many," so *polymer* means "many parts." There are many other polymers, which are found in everything from shoes to car bumpers. As you will see, many of the important molecules necessary for life are also polymers. Such molecules include DNA, glycogen, and proteins.

Alkynes

Hydrocarbons that contain one or more carbon-to-carbon triple bonds are called **alkynes**. The names of alkynes end in "-yne." Ethyne, commonly known as acetylene, is the simplest alkyne. It consists of two carbon atoms with a triple bond between them, with each carbon also bonded to one hydrogen atom. The chemical formula for ethyne is C_2H_2.

Alkynes are less common in nature than alkenes, but some are made naturally by some plants and bacteria. A few are used in drugs, including ethynyl estradiol, which is a synthetic female

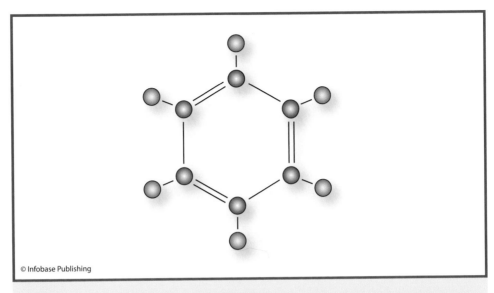

Figure 3.9 **The benzene molecule shown here is made up of a ring of six carbon atoms, with one hydrogen atom bonded to each carbon atom. Exposure to large amounts can be deadly.**

hormone used in birth control pills. Others have been tested as anticancer medications.

Acetylene, which is produced from coal or natural gas, is burned with oxygen in oxyacetylene torches for welding. This mixture of gases can reach temperatures of 5,072°F (2,800°C), which is hot enough to melt steel.

Aromatic Hydrocarbons

In **aromatic hydrocarbons**, the carbon atoms form a ring instead of being bonded together in a straight chain. The most common aromatic structure is the benzene ring, which consists of six carbon atoms bonded together in a hexagonal structure. Note that there are three double bonds.

The term "aromatic" was applied to these compounds because many of the first such compounds discovered had pleasant odors.

There are huge numbers of compounds containing benzene rings in which one or more of the hydrogens is replaced by another atom. This other atom may be a carbon that, in turn, is bonded to other carbons and even other ring structures.

OTHER KINDS OF ORGANIC COMPOUNDS

In addition to alkanes, alkenes, and alkynes, which have been described above, there are many kinds of organic compounds. The millions of different carbon compounds are divided into families according to their **functional groups**, which are atoms or groups of atoms that give the molecules their characteristic properties. Generally, the functional group replaces a hydrogen atom in a chain or ring of carbon atoms.

Alcohols

Consider ethane, the alkane with two carbon atoms and six attached hydrogen atoms. If one of the hydrogen atoms is replaced by an OH group, the result is ethyl alcohol, or ethanol, the alcohol portion of alcoholic beverages. The OH is the **alcohol** group. The names of alcohols end in "-ol." The structural formulas for ethane and ethyl alcohol are:

$$
\begin{array}{cc}
\text{H} \quad \text{H} & \text{H} \quad \textbf{OH} \\
| \quad\; | & | \quad\; | \\
\text{H} - \text{C} - \text{C} - \text{H} & \text{H} - \text{C} - \text{C} - \text{H} \\
| \quad\; | & | \quad\; | \\
\text{H} \quad \text{H} & \text{H} \quad \text{H} \\
\text{Ethane} & \text{Ethyl alcohol}
\end{array}
$$

During a chemical reaction, the OH group undergoes a change, forming new substances. The alcohols are an important group of organic compounds because they are widely used in disinfectants, cleaning solutions, antifreezes, and drugs.

Carbonyl Group

A **carbonyl group** consists of a carbon atom that is double-bonded to an oxygen atom, C = O. Carbonyl groups are parts of several other kinds of functional groups. A **carboxyl group** is a carbonyl bonded to an OH group, and an **ester** is a carbonyl bonded to an OR group (an R group can be anything except H).

Carboxyl Group

Carboxyl groups are found in carboxylic acids, which are organic acids. Carboxyl groups are the functional group in fatty acids, which react to form fats and lipids, and are one of the functional groups in **amino acids**, which are the building blocks of proteins. They are also present in soaps. Carboxyl groups consist of a carbon atom double-bonded to an oxygen atom and single-bonded to an OH group.

$$
\begin{array}{c}
O \\
\parallel \\
R - C - OH
\end{array}
$$

Esters

When a carboxylic acid reacts with an alcohol, the product is called an ester. Esters are made up of a carbon atom double-bonded to an oxygen atom and single bonded to an R group. The OH group of the carboxylic acid is replaced by an OR group.

$$
\begin{array}{c}
O \\
\parallel \\
R - C - OR
\end{array}
$$

Esters are known for their pleasant fragrances. Many flowers and fruits, including oranges, owe their fragrances to esters. Esters are used in perfumes and as flavorings in food and soft drinks.

Amines

In addition to carboxyl groups, amino acids have a second functional group, the **amine** group (NH_2). Amines are related to **ammonia** (NH_3).

A BASIC CHEMICAL REACTION

A **chemical reaction** is the process of changing one chemical substance into another. Chemical reactions begin with one set of substances and end with another set of substances. In the course of a chemical reaction, some chemical bonds are broken and others are formed. The substances at the beginning of the reaction are called the **reactants**, while the new substance or substances created by the reaction is called the **product**.

Chemists write the reactants and products as **chemical equations**. All chemical equations follow this format: Reactants → Products. Numbers indicate how much of each substance is needed or produced. The arrow indicates that a chemical reaction has taken place and something new has been created.

An example of a simple chemical reaction is the formation of water from hydrogen and oxygen. These two substances combine in the ratio of two hydrogen to one oxygen to create a new substance, water, which is the product. The chemical equation for the formation of water is:

$$2H_2 + O_2 \rightarrow 2H_2O.$$

Just as carbon atoms readily form bonds with other atoms, they readily participate in chemical reactions. Again, it is the chemistry of carbon compounds that makes them important participants in chemical reactions.

TYPES OF CHEMICAL REACTIONS

Three common types of chemical reactions are **substitution reactions**, **elimination reactions**, and **addition reactions**.

Understanding how functional groups behave in substitution and elimination reactions is key to understanding carbon chemistry.

Substitution Reactions

During a substitution reaction, two reactants exchange parts to form a new substance. If the groups are written as X and Y, a generic substitution reaction looks like this:

$$C—X + Y \rightarrow C—Y + X$$

The functional group, X, in the reactants is substituted for the group of atoms called Y during the chemical reaction and two new products (C—Y and X) are created.

Exactly how this chemical reaction occurs and how long it takes to unfold depends on the exact groups of atoms involved. Substitution reactions happen all the time in carbon chemistry.

Elimination Reactions

During an elimination reaction, atoms are removed, or eliminated, from adjacent carbons on a carbon chain, producing a small molecule, which is often water. A double bond forms between the adjacent carbons, producing an alkene. For example, ethyl alcohol (ethanol) can undergo an elimination reaction to form ethylene by the loss of H and OH, which form H_2O (water).

$$
\begin{array}{c}
\mathbf{H} \quad \mathbf{OH} \\
| \quad \; | \\
H — C — C — H \\
| \quad \; | \\
H \quad H \\
\text{Ethyl alcohol}
\end{array}
\rightarrow
\begin{array}{c}
H \quad H \\
| \quad \; | \\
C = C + \mathbf{H_2O} \\
| \quad \; | \\
H \quad H \\
\text{Ethylene} \quad \text{Water}
\end{array}
$$

Addition Reactions

In addition reactions, atoms are added, often to molecules that have carbon-carbon double or triple bonds. For example, two hydrogen atoms can be added to an ethylene molecule to produce ethane. In the process, the carbon-carbon double bond is converted to a single bond.

$$
\begin{array}{ccc}
\text{H} \quad \text{H} & & \text{H} \quad \text{H} \\
| \quad | & & | \quad | \\
\text{C} = \text{C} \ + \ \text{H} + \text{H} & \rightarrow & \text{H} - \text{C} - \text{C} - \text{H} \\
| \quad | & & | \quad | \\
\text{H} \quad \text{H} & & \text{H} \quad \text{H} \\
\text{Ethylene} & & \text{Ethane}
\end{array}
$$

Addition reactions are the opposite of elimination reactions.

The reactions discussed here are only a very small sample of the reactions of carbon compounds.

Biomolecules

Biomolecules are molecules found in living things. The major classes of biomolecules are **proteins**, **carbohydrates**, **fats**, and **nucleic acids**. All biomolecules contain carbon, hydrogen, and oxygen. Proteins also contain nitrogen and sometimes sulfur, and nucleic acids contain nitrogen and phosphorus. Other types of atoms may also be found in these compounds.

PROTEINS

Proteins are organic polymers made up of amino acids. They have both structural and functional roles in living organisms. For example, proteins are a major part of the structures of skin, hair, and nails. Special proteins within the cells of the body that are called enzymes are necessary for all the chemical reactions of life. Without enzymes, the chemical reactions inside cells would happen too slowly to support life.

The proteins found in living things contain any combination of twenty different amino acids. As mentioned previously, the functional groups of an amino acid are an amino group, NH_2, and a carboxyl group, COOH. The amino group is written as H_2N in this diagram to indicate that the carbon atom is bonded to the nitrogen atom of the amino group.

$$\text{(amino group) } H_2N - \underset{\underset{R}{|}}{\overset{\overset{H}{|}}{C}} - \overset{\overset{O}{||}}{C} - OH \text{ (carboxyl group)}$$

The R group, which can consist of varying numbers and kinds of atoms, is different in each of the twenty amino acids. The rest of the structure is the same.

The amino acids in proteins are linked together by bonds between the amino group of one amino acid and the carboxyl group of another. These bonds are called peptide bonds. When a peptide bond forms between two amino acids, one hydrogen and one oxygen atom are lost from the carboxyl group of one amino acid and one hydrogen atom is lost from the amino group of the other amino acid. These discarded atoms become a molecule of water (H_2O), leaving what is called a dipeptide, below.

$$H_2N - \underset{\underset{R}{|}}{\overset{\overset{H}{|}}{C}} - \underset{\underset{H}{|}}{\overset{\overset{O}{||}}{C}} - \underset{\underset{R'}{|}}{N} - \overset{\overset{H}{|}}{C} - \overset{\overset{O}{||}}{C} - OH \ (+ H_2O)$$

This structure is called a dipeptide because it shows a peptide bond linking two amino acids. However, the chain could have been made up of fifty or more amino acids, all linked by peptide bonds.

Such a chain is called a polypeptide because it is made up of many amino acids.

Proteins have several different levels of structure. The order of their constituent amino acids is only the first. The arrangement of the polypeptide backbone is the second level. Some common arrangements include a helix, which is like a coiled spring, and a pleated sheet. The third level of structure involves the folding of the protein. The huge number of different arrangements for the twenty different amino acids and the variety of ways that the protein can be shaped allows for an almost infinite variety of proteins.

CARBOHYDRATES

Carbohydrates are a large class of carbon compounds that have many OH groups on adjacent carbon atoms and one $C=O$ group. Carbohydrates include sugars, starch, cellulose, and glycogen, to name a few. The group was named after the discovery that the formula for glucose and some other sugars was $C_6H_{12}O_6$, which made it seem that the group consisted of carbon and water—$C_6(H_2O)_6$.

HANDEDNESS IN MOLECULES

Some amino acids and carbohydrates have so-called "right-handed" and "left-handed" structures. This has to do with the arrangement of their atoms. This handedness happens when there are four different groups bonded to one carbon atom. The right- and left-handed forms are mirror images of each other. Although their chemical properties are identical, it is interesting to note that only one of the forms of amino acids is biologically active: the left-handed form.

Carbohydrates are divided into three groups called monosaccharides, disaccharides, and polysaccharides. The monosaccharides are the simple sugars, like glucose. The disaccharides, which are composed of two monosaccharides bonded together, include sucrose, or table sugar. The polysaccharides are polymers of monosaccharides and include starch and cellulose, which are both made from glucose.

Carbohydrates serve a number of different functions in living organisms. Glucose, for example, is broken down for energy in most living things. Starch and glycogen, which are polymers of glucose, are energy storage compounds. An organism converts any leftover glucose into starch (in plants) or glycogen (in animals). These substances, called polysaccharides, are broken down when glucose is needed for energy.

GLUCOSE AND DIABETES

The ability of human body cells to use glucose for energy requires the ability of the glucose to pass out of the blood and into the cells through the membrane surrounding each cell. This is made possible by a substance called insulin, which is made by the pancreas. Insulin is a hormone, a substance that is secreted directly into the blood and that acts only on specific target tissues.

Without insulin, glucose produced by the digestion of food remains in the blood and is excreted from the body by the kidneys. This is what happens in people with untreated diabetes. Not everyone who has diabetes suffers from a shortage of insulin. Sometimes the body produces enough insulin, but the cells have become insensitive to it, causing the glucose to remain in the blood. Obesity and lack of exercise are two factors that can contribute to the occurrence of diabetes.

LIPIDS

Lipids are a class of biomolecules defined by the fact that they are insoluble in water and similar solvents. Lipids include the fats in foods and the fats stored in our bodies, waxes, and steroids. Importantly for the body, the membranes that surround all cells are made of lipids. Like the carbohydrates starch and glycogen, lipids also serve as energy storage compounds, but per gram, lipids contain more than twice as much energy as carbohydrates and proteins. Excess nutrients not needed for energy are stored as body fat.

The most familiar naturally occurring fats are made up of glycerol (also called glycerine) and fatty acids. Such fats are called triacylglycerols. They include solid animal fats, such as butter and lard, and liquid vegetable oils, such as olive, peanut, and corn oil. Glycerol is the three-carbon compound that reacts with fatty acids to form fats. Fatty acids are long chains of carbon atoms with hydrogen and oxygen atoms attached. The fatty acid chains sometimes include double bonds between the carbon atoms. Fats that contain no double bonds are called saturated fats, because they cannot add any hydrogen atoms. Fats that do contain double bonds are called unsaturated fats because they can bond with additional hydrogen atoms. (Two hydrogens can be added at each double bond, which leaves a single bond between the carbon atoms.)

Diets high in saturated fats are considered unhealthy because of the danger of developing fatty deposits in the arteries, particularly the arteries of the heart. On the other hand, the intake of limited amounts of unsaturated vegetable oils is actually considered beneficial.

NUCLEIC ACIDS

Nucleic acids are organic polymers that carry hereditary information, which in turn directs the synthesis of all the proteins in the body. There are two nucleic acids—**deoxyribonucleic acid (DNA)** and **ribonucleic acid (RNA)**.

DNA is found in the nucleus of cells. In a cell that is not dividing, the DNA is in a dispersed form called **chromatin**. When the cell is preparing to divide, the chromatin reorganizes itself, forming pairs of thick, rodlike chromosomes. Chromosomes consist of DNA and protein. The **genes**, which control heredity, are positioned along the DNA in the chromosomes. Each gene consists of a specific section of DNA and directs the synthesis of a specific protein.

DNA has the unusual ability to make exact copies of itself, a process called replication. It is this ability that allows the hereditary information to be passed from one generation to the next.

Both DNA and RNA are polymers made up of subunits called nucleotides. The nucleotides in DNA consist of the monosaccharide (simple sugar) deoxyribose, phosphate groups (PO_4), and one of four different nitrogen bases. These bases, which are ring compounds, are adenine (A), cytosine (C), guanine (G), and thymine (T). The nucleotides in RNA consist of the monosaccharide ribose, phosphate groups, and one of four nitrogen bases. As in DNA, the nitrogen bases include adenine, cytosine, and guanine, but instead of thymine, there is a different base, uracil (U). Thus, the structures of DNA and RNA nucleotides differ in the sugar they contain and in one of the four nitrogen bases. The other major difference is that DNA is a double-stranded molecule, while RNA consists of a single strand.

The hereditary information, or **genetic code**, resides in the order of the nucleotides in DNA. This information is copied from the DNA in the cell nucleus into molecules of a special RNA, which passes out of the nucleus to the sites of protein synthesis. Here, the code copied into the RNA determines which proteins are synthesized. These, in turn, determine the structure and functions of the cells and of the organism as a whole.

Both the process of replication and the copying of the genetic code into molecules of RNA depend on base pairing. The nitrogen bases in the nucleotides of DNA and RNA pair in a specific way. In

DNA, adenine (A) pairs with thymine (T) and cytosine (C) pairs with guanine (G). Therefore, when there is an A in one strand of the double-stranded DNA molecule, there is a T in the other strand. When the genetic code is copied from DNA to RNA, the two strands of DNA molecule separate, and the RNA nucleotides pair with nucleotides on each strand of DNA. In this case, the nucleotide that pairs with adenine (A) on the DNA is uracil (U) because RNA does not contain thymine (T). Because of the exact nature of base pairing, the genetic code can be transmitted accurately at each stage of the process.

Now that carbon has been discussed on an atomic level, it is time to explore the behavior and roles of the element carbon and of carbon compounds in nature.

The Carbon Cycle

Carbon is the fourth most abundant element in the universe. It is a key component of the atmosphere, sea, land, and all living things on Earth. In one form or another, carbon is recycled constantly between the oceans, land, air, and living things. The processes that move carbon atoms on Earth collectively make up the **carbon cycle**.

Each part of the carbon cycle acts as a reservoir for carbon atoms: a place where carbon enters, resides for some time, and then leaves. Each reservoir has its own characteristics. The amount of carbon present, the length of time carbon remains, the way carbon enters and exits, and the reactions and roles of carbon atoms vary for each reservoir.

The **biosphere** is the part of Earth that contains living things. This includes all inhabitable parts of the atmosphere, the sea, and the land. Because all living things are made of carbon, all of the

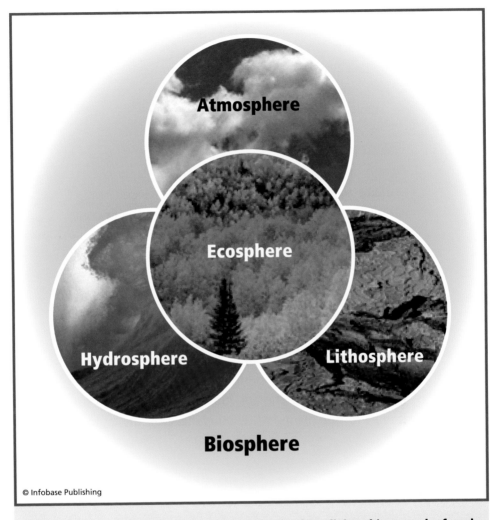

Figure 5.1   The biosphere is the area of Earth where living things can be found. The biosphere is made up of the land, water, air, and living organisms.

parts of the biosphere that contain living things also contain large amounts of carbon. Earth's biosphere contains about 1,900 giga-tons of carbon. One **gigaton** (Gt) is equal to one billion metric tons (about equal to the weight of 142 million African elephants or 2,750 Empire State Buildings).

PROCESSES OF THE CARBON CYCLE

The cycling of carbon through the atmosphere, oceans, land, and living things involves the following processes: photosynthesis, respiration, burning, burial of organic matter, decomposition, and weathering.

Photosynthesis

Photosynthesis is the process by which plants use energy from sunlight to convert carbon dioxide (CO_2) and water (H_2O) to carbohydrates. Both the carbon dioxide and water come from the environment. Photosynthesis is the main process that removes carbon dioxide from the atmosphere. Oxygen and water vapor are released into the atmosphere as by-products of the reactions of photosynthesis.

Photosynthesis begins with the green pigment, chlorophyll. Electrons in the chlorophyll absorb energy from sunlight. Through a complex series of reactions, this energy is used to synthesize carbohydrates. These carbohydrates, directly or indirectly, are the source of all food energy for animals on Earth. Some animals feed directly on the plants, while others feed on the animals that feed on plants.

Respiration

Respiration is the process that living organisms use to break down nutrients, mainly the sugar glucose, to create energy. This process requires oxygen. The energy released by respiration goes into the synthesis of a compound called adenosine triphosphate (ATP). The ATP, in turn, is used to provide the needed energy for all of the reactions of metabolism (meaning all the chemical reactions in an organism). The waste products of respiration are carbon dioxide and water vapor, which pass out of the organism and into the atmosphere. They are in the air exhaled from the lungs of humans and other animals.

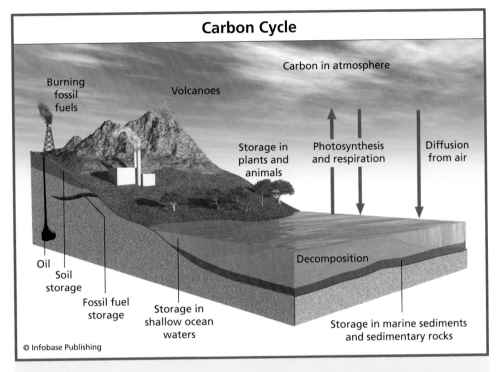

Carbon Cycle

Carbon in atmosphere

Burning fossil fuels

Volcanoes

Storage in plants and animals

Photosynthesis and respiration

Diffusion from air

Oil

Soil storage

Fossil fuel storage

Storage in shallow ocean waters

Decomposition

Storage in marine sediments and sedimentary rocks

© Infobase Publishing

Figure 5.2   The carbon cycle is the exchange of carbon between the air, water, land, and animals. The movement of carbon atoms in this cycle can take millions of years.

Weathering

Weathering is the process by which rock is broken down into smaller and smaller particles. It involves both mechanical and chemical breakdowns. The mechanical breakdown into smaller and smaller pieces occurs as a result of exposure to freeze-thaw cycles and to the action of wind and water. Chemical breakdown occurs as a result of exposure to air and water and other chemicals that may be dissolved in water, such as acids. Weathering by exposure to atmosphere results in some of the carbon dioxide being removed from the atmosphere along with the broken-down rock and eventually washed into the ocean.

Decomposition and the Formation of Fossil Fuels

Decomposition, or rotting, occurs when bacteria and other decay organisms, or **decomposers**, break down the remains of dead plants and animals into simpler compounds. Without these organisms, the material in the remains of dead plants and animals would not be recycled. When there is adequate oxygen, the decomposition process can continue until the material is broken down completely. The carbon compounds in the decaying organism are converted to carbon dioxide and water vapor. When oxygen is missing, the process cannot proceed past a certain point, and much of the chemical energy in the original material is left in the partially decomposed remains. These energy-rich remains in their various forms are known as **fossil fuels**, and are the major source of energy for human civilization.

Coal

Coal was formed from the remains of plants in a swampy environment. The plants were probably giant tree ferns, which are now extinct. When the plants died, they were covered by water and waterlogged soil, as well as by leaves and other plant parts. The rotting vegetation used up the oxygen in the water, which slowed decomposition. Further deaths produced more layers of rotting plants, with the upper layers covering and protecting the lower layers from exposure to air. Over thousands of years, the weight of the overlying sediments forced out the water and gases from the rotting plant material. This partial decomposition very gradually produced peat, which is a brown and porous mass of organic matter. Peat still contains recognizable plant parts. The peat was covered by more layers of dead plants. Further pressure, heat, and chemical change converted peat to a soft, coal-like material called lignite. The lignite, in turn, was converted to soft coal, and sometimes hard coal, by further burial and the effects of pressure and heat. Due to the absence of oxygen under these conditions, these products of partially decayed organic material retain a great amount of chemical energy that would otherwise have decomposed into carbon dioxide and water vapor.

Oil and Natural Gas

Oil and natural gas, like coal, formed from the remains of living things under conditions where oxygen was lacking and there was pressure and heat. Whereas coal was formed mainly from the remains of plants, oil and natural gas were formed from the remains of all kinds of organisms, mostly in coastal areas. The sediments on the ocean floor do not contain much oxygen, thus the remains of various dead organisms decompose slowly. Overlying layers added pressure and heat, and over millions of years some of the overlying sediments was converted to rock, and some of the buried organic matter was converted to liquid petroleum and natural gas. Because petroleum and natural gas are light, they rise in water until they become trapped by rock or some other impermeable layer.

CARBON IN THE ATMOSPHERE

The atmosphere contains about 750 gigatons of carbon, mostly in the form of carbon dioxide. Although 750 gigatons is a huge amount of material, it is not a great amount when compared to other reservoirs in the carbon cycle.

Carbon enters the atmosphere mainly as the result of respiration and burning of any kind. The oceans provide a slower, smaller pathway for carbon to enter the atmosphere. Dissolved carbon dioxide moves through the ocean's waters in currents. At some places on the planet, mainly near the equator, currents bring cold water rich in carbon dioxide from deep in the ocean to the sea surface, where the Sun warms it. These warm surface waters naturally release carbon dioxide into the atmosphere.

CARBON IN THE OCEANS

The oceans on Earth contain a lot of the planet's carbon—about 39,000 Gt. The majority of this carbon exists as **inorganic carbon** atoms, which is carbon that does not come from living things. The two main forms of carbon in the sea are carbon dioxide and

FIRE

Fire is one of the processes that moves carbon around Earth. Often it spreads undesirable carbon-based air pollution. Smoke is made mostly of tiny particles of carbon. When a forest or any other fuel source burns, some of the carbon contained in the trees, plants, and organic matter is converted to carbon dioxide (CO_2), but some is transformed into airborne carbon, or smoke. While naturally-occurring forest fires have served as a crucial component of the carbon cycle by moving carbon back into Earth's atmosphere, the extra carbon unloaded by vast, human-made fires for land-clearing purposes puts this process into overdrive. The widespread burning of tropical forests to clear the land for farming contributes large amounts of carbon to the atmosphere, both as smoke and as carbon dioxide. In addition, the loss of these important forests cuts down on the removal of carbon dioxide from the air and on the generation of oxygen.

bicarbonate ions (HCO_3^-). Bicarbonate ions are created when carbon dioxide molecules dissolved in seawater undergo a chemical reaction and combine with hydrogen. About 88% of the inorganic carbon in the sea is made up of bicarbonate ions.

Together, carbon dioxide and bicarbonate ions affect the acidity, or **pH**, of seawater. The pH is a measure of hydrogen ion (H^+) concentration in a liquid. When carbon dioxide combines with hydrogen, it changes the amounts of hydrogen ions in the water and alters the pH.

In a way, the oceans are carbon's temporary resting place during the carbon cycle. Carbon atoms can stay in the oceans for several hundred years before returning to the atmosphere and continuing through the carbon cycle.

How Carbon Enters the Oceans

Carbon dioxide mainly enters the oceans from the atmosphere. It dissolves in the cold surface waters around the north and south poles. When these cold waters sink, they carry the carbon deep into the oceans where it can be stored for hundreds of years. Because of their ability to store carbon, the oceans are known as a **carbon sink**. The sea as a carbon sink has become increasingly important in recent decades because human activity is adding increasing amounts of carbon dioxide to the atmosphere, and much of it ends up in the sea. According to the National Aeronautics and Space Administration (NASA), almost half of the carbon added to the atmosphere by fossil fuel burning ends up sequestered in the ocean.

Although the oceans are a natural sink for carbon, scientists are also exploring the idea of using the sea to store excess carbon produced by humans. If carbon dioxide could be collected and contained, scientists suggest, it could be injected into the deep oceans for long-term storage. Here, the carbon dioxide would either dissolve into seawater or form giant, underwater carbon dioxide lakes. Either way, the excess carbon would not return to the atmosphere for a long time.

How Carbon Exits the Oceans

Carbon dioxide mainly exits the oceans at the interface with the atmosphere. Warm surface waters easily release carbon dioxide into the atmosphere. When warm waters rise to the surface, mainly near the equator, carbon dioxide is transferred from the water to the air. Because of this, the sea is a source of carbon for the carbon cycle as well as a carbon sink.

On a much smaller, faster scale, photosynthesizing algae, which are one-celled or multicellular organisms living in the ocean, take in dissolved carbon dioxide just as plants do on land and use it in the synthesis of carbohydrates. Like land plants, they also give off oxygen. Although sea, or marine, organisms remove huge amounts of carbon dioxide from the atmosphere, the amount is still much less than the total carbon dioxide released into the atmosphere.

CARBON IN THE LAND

The land, which includes the soils on the surface of Earth as well as the rocks and sediments deep in the ground and under the oceans, contains most of the carbon in the carbon cycle. The rocks under Earth's surface hold about 65 million Gt of carbon; the soils on the surface hold over 1,500 Gt of carbon. Underground, much of the carbon is in fossil fuels—coal, oil, and natural gas.

At the surface, much of the carbon exists in rocks, such as limestone. Limestone is made of calcium carbonate ($CaCO_3$). It can be found in sediment deposits along rivers and roads; it is also the main ingredient in seashells.

Earth's land reservoirs play an important role in long-term carbon storage. In fact, they store carbon for very long periods of time. The carbon in limestone, for example, may remain in a land reservoir for thousands of years. The carbon in a fossil fuel may be stored for millions of years.

While the land holds the least active carbon atoms in the carbon cycle, it also holds the most economically valuable carbon atoms in the carbon cycle. Humans have long looked to the land as a source of carbon for fuel. Because land carbon is an important human resource, it is important to understand the way carbon enters and exits the Earth's crust.

How Carbon Enters the Land

Carbon enters the land in many different ways. Most of these processes take place over very long periods of time and create very large sources of carbon.

Most carbon was incorporated into the rocky Earth when the planet was formed, about 4.5 billion years ago. Since then, Earth's carbon has been redistributed by the different parts of the carbon cycle. Today, smaller amounts of carbon enter the land through the decomposition of the remains of living things. When something dies, its body (and all the carbon in it) eventually decomposes. Over millions of years, some of the carbon compounds from the remains may be buried far enough underground that heat and pressure convert the carbon compounds into coal, oil, or natural gas.

CARBON EMISSIONS

Most of the carbon added to the atmosphere by human activity is from the burning of fossil fuels for energy. In the past 50 years, the amount of carbon produced by human activities each year has steadily increased. Current emissions, measured in Gt, are over four times greater than they were in the 1950s and 1960s according to *Vital Signs 2007-2008*, a report from the World Watch Institute, an independent research organization. This is largely due to the growing human population and its increased energy needs.

TABLE 5.1 CARBON EMISSIONS

YEAR	CARBON EMISSIONS FROM FOSSIL FUEL BURNING (Gt)
1950	1.61
1960	2.53
1970	4.00
1975	4.52
1980	5.21
1985	5.30
1990	5.99
1995	6.21
2000	6.45
2005	7.56

CARBON RESERVOIRS

Each reservoir in Earth's carbon cycle has its own size and length of storage time. Some reservoirs hold lots of carbon for long periods of time, while other reservoirs hold smaller amounts of carbon for shorter periods of time. Here are the reservoirs at a glance.

TABLE 5.2 CARBON RESERVOIRS

LOCATION	AMOUNT OF CARBON (Gt)	LENGTH OF STORAGE TIME
Rocks underground	65,000,000	Millions of years
Oceans	39,000	Hundreds of years
Living things	1,900	Minutes, days, and lifetimes
Surface soils	1,580	Thousands of years
Atmosphere	750	Hundreds of years

Sources: http://www.ldeo.columbia.edu/edu/dees/V1003/lectures/global_carbon_cycle/index.html and http://en.wikipedia.org/wiki/Carbon_cycle#In_the_biosphere

How Carbon Exits the Land

Carbon exits the land in many different ways, some of them natural and some the result of human activity. Either way, however, carbon does not easily leave the land.

Volcanic explosions and the weathering of rocks are two ways carbon naturally leaves the land. When a volcano erupts, it releases material such as carbon-containing gases and rocks. The eruption moves the carbon from the land to the atmosphere. The carbon contained in rocks on Earth's surface is released when weathering occurs.

When it comes to human activity, mining is the main way carbon leaves the land. Humans regularly extract fossil fuel carbon to burn for energy; we mine the mountains for coal, pump oil out of the ground, and collect natural gas from under the ground and under the sea floor. Currently, humans are extracting fossil fuels faster than the Earth can replace them.

CARBON IN LIVING THINGS

When added up, all the living things on Earth contain about 1,900 Gt of carbon. All the cells in living organisms are made of carbon compounds, and the many kinds of molecules they contain that are used in life processes are also carbon compounds.

The role of living things in the carbon cycle is primarily to move carbon atoms around (rather than to store carbon for long periods of time). Living things absorb carbon from the atmosphere, the sea, and the Earth and transform it into new forms as the remains of dead organisms are added to the sea and land.

Understanding how carbon enters and exits living things is just the beginning of understanding how much life on Earth depends on carbon.

How Carbon Enters and Exits Living Things

Living organisms move carbon atoms by eating, breathing, and reproducing—in other words, simply by being alive. Through these life processes, carbon enters a living thing in one form and exits in another form. When humans eat, for example, carbon enters the body. Fruit, vegetables, and meat are made mostly of carbon. These foods are broken down to release energy that the body needs. They also supply needed nutrients. The food material that is not incorporated into the cells of the body exits the body as wastes, which include exhaled carbon dioxide. When organisms die, their remains are broken down by decay, most commonly in soil. Nutrients released by the breakdown of larger compounds can also be used by other organisms. Carbon dioxide and water vapor are also products of decay.

DEVELOPING CARBON SINKS

Carbon sinks are reservoirs that store carbon atoms and molecules. Earth has many natural carbon sinks that are part of the planet's carbon cycle, including the oceans, ice sheets, the rocks that make up part of Earth's crust, and forests. But as the amount of atmospheric carbon increases from human activity, scientists are looking for additional carbon sinks.

One way to increase Earth's ability to store carbon is by beefing up the existing, natural carbon sinks. Forests, for example, already take in about 10% of the atmospheric carbon produced in the United States, according to the Environmental Protection Agency. By planting more forests, humans could increase the planet's ability to take in atmospheric carbon in the future. Such programs have already been implemented on small scales throughout the world to help offset the excess atmospheric carbon being produced.

Likewise, the ability of the oceans to take in atmospheric carbon could be increased. Algae, plankton, and other organisms carry on photosynthesis as do green plants on land: They take in carbon dioxide and release oxygen. In fact, about half of the oxygen we breathe is produced by these organisms. Experiments to fertilize plankton growth in the oceans have already been completed, but the method has not yet been implemented as a way to increase the ocean's carbon contents.

Another way to increase Earth's ability to store carbon is by creating new, artificial carbon sinks that would trap excess carbon gas produced by human activity before it enters the atmosphere. The carbon dioxide would be collected and placed in a new location for controllable, long-term storage. Scientists have already experimented with two new carbon sink locations, one deep in the ocean, the other underground. In each case, carbon is forcefully injected into its new reservoir for long-term storage.

In the ocean experiments, scientists pump carbon dioxide into the deep ocean, where it forms giant lakes of liquid carbon dioxide. Eventually, the carbon dioxide dissolves into the surrounding waters. However, it is unclear how such increased amounts of oceanic carbon would affect sea life and water chemistry.

In the underground experiments, scientists inject carbon dioxide into spaces deep in the Earth. Some of these underground spaces are caves or old mines; others are empty holes that once held oil or natural gas. Oil companies have practiced these storage methods for decades because they are relatively inexpensive and easy, and can also enrich existing oil reserves. But so far, no company or government has officially adopted this method for long-term carbon storage.

SUMMARY OF THE CARBON CYCLE

In the course of the carbon cycle, carbon moves from the atmosphere, where it mostly exists in the form of carbon dioxide, into biological molecules—the molecules that make up living things and the wastes and remains. The incorporation of atmospheric carbon into living organisms begins with the process of photosynthesis. Some atmospheric carbon dioxide is also removed from the atmosphere when it dissolves in the cold ocean waters at the north and south poles.

Carbon is released into the atmosphere as carbon dioxide as part of the process of respiration. The decomposition of the remains and wastes of living things by bacteria and other soil organisms also releases carbon dioxide into the atmosphere. In addition, carbon dioxide is released into the atmosphere by fires and other types of burning, including the burning of fossil fuels and erupting volcanoes.

Some of the carbon released by decomposition may be washed into rivers and the ocean. Some of it may be taken up by other living things for use in their life processes. Some of it may be buried in sediments and, over long periods of time, converted to fossil fuels. The burial and conversion of carbon compounds to fossil fuels upsets the balance between photosynthesis and respiration because these processes remove the carbon from the cycle for such long periods of time. Some carbon is also removed from the cycle for longs periods of time when the shells of some small ocean-dwelling

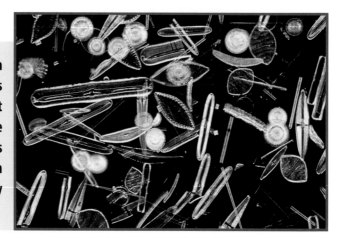

Figure 5.3 Plankton are microscopic plants and animals that drift in bodies of water. There are many different forms of plankton. Plankton are the first link in many food chains.

organisms sink to the ocean floor and are converted to limestone by the pressure of overlying sediments. The carbon from limestone returns to the cycle when the limestone erodes.

If photosynthesis and respiration worked in perfect balance, all of the carbon dioxide produced by respiration and other processes would be taken up by plants and other photosynthesizing organisms; all of the oxygen produced by photosynthesis would be taken up by animals and other organisms that use oxygen for respiration. However, this isn't the case. Although the concentration of carbon dioxide in the atmosphere is less than 0.5 of 1%, the concentration of oxygen is almost 21%. This excess oxygen in the atmosphere is counterbalanced by the buried carbon, organic matter in sediments, and in fossil fuels.

With time, some of this carbon-containing material in sediments is exposed by erosion, weathering, and other natural processes. Large amounts of the carbon-containing materials are exposed by human activities, such as mining coal and digging oil wells. Whenever coal and oil are burned, the carbon dioxide is added back to the air and this tends toward restoring the photosynthesis/respiration balance. However, this is a balance that is not to our advantage, since we cannot live without the "excess" oxygen in the air that the current imbalance provides.

LIFE WITHOUT CARBON

All life on Earth is based on the element carbon. This means that in living organisms on Earth, body structures and the chemicals that take part in life processes are almost all carbon compounds. But scientists and science fiction enthusiasts alike have long speculated on the possibility that elsewhere in the universe there could be life forms based on other elements, particularly silicon.

Science fiction books and television shows have fueled the life-form debate by creating a number of imaginary, silicon-based creatures. The Horta, perhaps one of the most well-known creatures, first appeared in 1967 on an episode of the original *Star Trek* series. These intelligent, silicon-based life forms looked a little like burnt marshmallows, yet intelligently defended their store of eggs against the unaware human invaders.

Silicon is chemically similar to carbon. An atom of silicon, like an atom of carbon, has four electrons in its outermost shell, and these electrons are available for forming chemical bonds. Like carbon, silicon can bond with four other elements to create a huge range of different compounds. This fact alone, some say, makes silicon a possible backbone for biological molecules. However, a more detailed examination raises doubts about the ability of silicon to form the kinds of structures necessary to build or sustain any form of life as we know it.

Carbon can form double and triple bonds and a large variety of structures, including long chains with and without branches and five- and six-membered rings. Silicon, on the other hand, has a much more limited ability to form different structures because it is less easily capable of forming double and triple bonds. While carbon atoms often join by the tens of thousands, the largest silicon molecule ever observed in nature contained only six silicon atoms. Without the ability to form large, silicon-based structures, the chance of there being silicon-based life forms seems unlikely or at least very slight.

Silicon compounds also differ from carbon compounds in their "handedness." Many biologically important carbon compounds have both right-handed and left-handed structures, which refers to the way the atoms in the compounds are organized. Only one of these structures is biologically active. Silicon, on the other hand, most often does not display handedness of any

continues

continued

kind. Because life is so dependent on the specifics of chemistry, NASA scientists say, silicon-based life just will not work.

Another disadvantage of silicon-based life as compared to carbon-based life is the relatively low amount of silicon in the universe. While silicon is actually more abundant on Earth than carbon (it is the second most abundant element after oxygen), it is far less abundant throughout the universe.

The bottom line is that speculation about silicon-based life forms may make good television entertainment, but not good science. Experts at NASA's Astrobiology Institute say silicon-based life is not likely for two reasons. First, silicon chemistry just does not work like carbon chemistry; and, second, there is not much silicon in the universe.

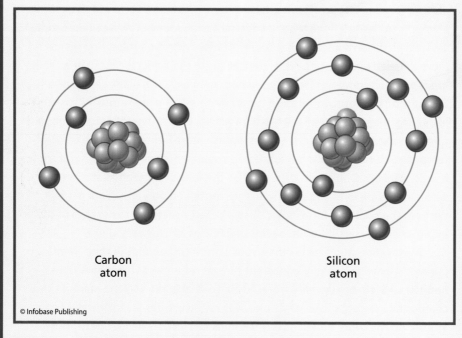

Carbon
atom

Silicon
atom

© Infobase Publishing

Figure 5.4   A carbon atom is less complex than a silicon atom.

The Atmosphere and Climate

The chemistry of Earth's **climate** is complicated. No one fully understands the relationship between the chemistry of the atmosphere and the resulting climate, but we do know that the chemical ingredients of the atmosphere—mainly the carbon content—have a direct effect on the temperature of the planet. The trick is figuring out exactly how the various ingredients interact with each other to produce the planet's climate over time.

THE ATMOSPHERE

The atmosphere of modern Earth is thought to be very different from that of early Earth. Scientists conjecture that Earth's first atmosphere consisted of carbon dioxide, water vapor, nitrogen, and hydrogen sulfide, with trace amounts of ammonia and methane. The gases in the atmosphere are thought to have been released from the interior of the planet by volcanic eruptions. At this early stage, Earth was very hot, with a molten core surrounded by a thin solid crust. The atmosphere contained no free oxygen.

The atmosphere of modern Earth is much different. Not accounting for a variable amount of water vapor, it consists of about 78.1% nitrogen, 20.9% oxygen, 0.93% argon, and just 0.038% carbon dioxide. It is thought that the argon originated from the radioactive decay of a potassium isotope deep within the Earth and was brought to the surface through geological events, where it diffused into the atmosphere. Because it is a stable element—it does not easily react or combine with other elements to form compounds—the amount of argon in the atmosphere remains constant. The high levels of nitrogen likely resulted from gas released by volcanic eruptions as Earth formed, as described above.

Nitrogen is essential to life on Earth because it is a component of amino acids and proteins. Plants require nitrogen, and fertilizers are sometimes used to supply extra nitrogen. Like carbon, nitrogen is recycled among the atmosphere, living things, and Earth. Most living things cannot use atmospheric nitrogen for their life processes. Instead, for them, nitrogen is converted to useable compounds by various bacteria. These compounds are taken up by plants and pass to animals when they eat the plants. The breakdown of dead plants and animals releases free nitrogen to the atmosphere. This process is also accomplished by the action of bacteria.

Before the appearance of photosynthetic organisms, there was no free oxygen in the atmosphere. Oxygen accumulated slowly as the numbers of photosynthesizing green algae and plants increased.

Photosynthesis and respiration help to maintain the concentrations of oxygen and carbon dioxide in the atmosphere. Respiration is the process by which carbohydrates (most commonly glucose) are broken down for the release of energy needed for life processes. Photosynthesis uses carbon dioxide and produces oxygen. Respiration does the opposite—it uses oxygen and produces carbon dioxide. Plants and algae carry on photosynthesis, while animals carry

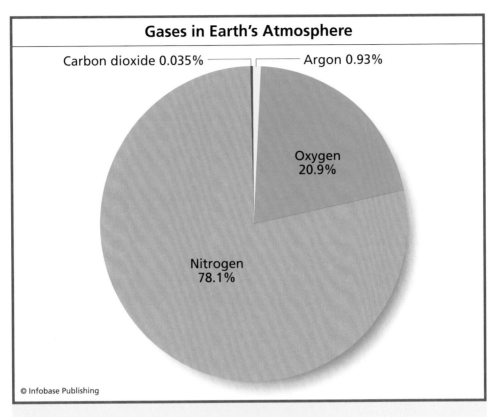

Gases in Earth's Atmosphere

Carbon dioxide 0.035% —— Argon 0.93%

Oxygen
20.9%

Nitrogen
78.1%

© Infobase Publishing

Figure 6.1 There are four main gases found on Earth.

on respiration. Photosynthetic organisms also carry on respiration, but they can use the products of respiration (carbon dioxide and water vapor) for photosynthesis and the products of photosynthesis (glucose and oxygen) for respiration. In the dark, when no photosynthesis occurs, plants may take in oxygen and release carbon dioxide.

In summary, Earth did not always have the same concentrations of atmospheric carbon dioxide and oxygen that it has today. The amounts of these gases in Earth's atmosphere changed as life on Earth evolved. As photosynthesizing organisms evolved, they developed the ability to capture energy from sunlight and use it to synthesize carbohydrates from atmospheric carbon dioxide. The release of oxygen as a by-product of this process eventually changed the make-up of the atmosphere to the point that the atmosphere of modern Earth contains about 21% oxygen.

This co-evolution of life, atmospheric carbon dioxide and oxygen levels, and a relatively moderate climate (compared with other planets) make Earth unique. Earth has far less atmospheric carbon dioxide than Mars and Venus, neighboring planets that were formed at about the same time. The atmospheres of both Mars and Venus are made of more than 95% carbon dioxide. On these planets, there are no photosynthesizing life forms to alter the levels of atmospheric carbon dioxide or to produce oxygen.

CLIMATE

Earth's climate is different than Earth's weather. **Weather** includes those atmospheric conditions that change from hour to hour or day to day, such as temperature, rain, wind speed, or cloud cover. Climate, on the other hand, is weather over time, the long-term patterns or trends in worldwide temperature, rain, and cloud cover, among other conditions. It is a worldwide look at weather averaged over thousands of years.

The climate of all the planets, including Earth, depends heavily on the atmosphere's carbon content. Only in recent decades have scientists realized that seemingly small changes in the level of carbon dioxide in Earth's atmosphere can create long-term, significant changes in climate. As a result, much research (and research money) has gone into learning about the chemistry of Earth's atmosphere and how this has influenced past and present climate conditions. The Earth's climate has not always been as it is today, and the carbon content of the atmospere has not always been as it is today, either.

Earth's Past Climate

Scientists know the carbon dioxide content of Earth's atmosphere has changed over time. They also know that Earth's climate has changed over time, sometimes in drastic ways. What they do not know is exactly how it all happens.

There have been roughly five periods in Earth's history where much of the planet was covered in ice. Global climate cooled for millions of years. The sheets of ice at the north and south poles of the planets grew to cover the oceans. The amount of CO_2 in the atmosphere dropped. These periods are widely known as **ice ages**. Atmospheric carbon dioxide dropped by about 25% during each major ice age. The drop in atmospheric carbon dioxide happened at the same time that global climate got colder. There just wasn't enough carbon dioxide to trap heat from the Sun and keep the planet's surface warm.

What scientists cannot determine is what caused carbon dioxide levels to drop in the first place during these icy periods in Earth's history. Some suggest perhaps photosynthesizing plants became too successful and took in too much carbon dioxide, causing less heat to be trapped near the planet's surface and consequently cooling the globe. Thus, while it is known cold climates coincide with low levels of atmospheric carbon dioxide, it is not known why.

Earth's Present Climate

The last big ice age on Earth ended about 12,000 years ago. Today, most scientists believe we are still coming out of that cold period into an **interglacial period**. An interglacial period is the time between ice ages when Earth is relatively warm. But just as scientists cannot determine why ice ages begin, they cannot determine why they end, either. It is only known that when carbon dioxide levels rise, the Earth starts to get warm.

The evolution of the current interglacial period is different from its predecessors in that it was during this time that humans evolved. They learned to use tools, manage fire, hunt, gather, and assert some control over their immediate environment. Through this evolution, they started to move carbon in different ways as well. When humans learned to burn and manage fire, they started to add carbon dioxide to the atmosphere.

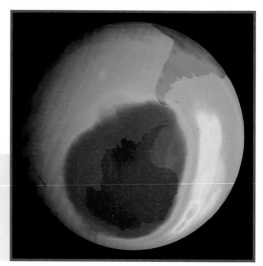

Figure 6.2   The hole in the ozone layer is represented in purple here.

Climate and Greenhouse Gases

Carbon dioxide is only one of the gases that cause Earth to warm. These so-called **greenhouse gases** also include methane (CH_4); ozone (O_3); nitrous oxide (N_2O); water vapor; and **chlorofluorocarbons** (**CFCs**), which are used as coolants in refrigerators and air conditioners. They are called "greenhouse" gases because they act like the glass of a greenhouse, which blocks the escape of heat and keeps the interior warm. The greenhouse gases act to keep heat trapped close to Earth's surface instead of allowing it to escape into the upper atmosphere. Carbon dioxide is the most important of the greenhouse gases. Its concentration in the atmosphere has increased by about 25% in the last 100 years, and it is still climbing unchecked. Under natural conditions, the greenhouse gases keep Earth warm enough for human life, therefore, the loss of the greenhouse gases would cause cooling of Earth's surface, which would also be a problem. Ozone, one of the greenhouse gases in the upper atmosphere, blocks some of the Sun's ultraviolet rays from reaching Earth's surface. These rays are damaging to human skin and eyes; ozone thus serves an important protective function.

Most of the carbon in the atmosphere exists as carbon dioxide, but carbon also occurs in other natural gases, including carbon monoxide (CO) and methane (CH_4). Synthetic gases, such as chlorofluorocarbons (CFCs), are also carbon-based atmospheric gases that affect climate.

QUICK CLIMATE CHANGE

Researchers at the Lamont-Doherty Earth Observatory (LDEO) at Columbia University in New York are studying the occurrence and causes of abrupt climate change.

Traditionally, scientists have assumed that climate change is a slow process, taking place over thousands of years. But researchers studying the planet's climate history are discovering that global temperatures can change very abruptly—as much as 18°F (10°C) in 10 years in one example. This temperature change is so fast that human society would not have enough time to adapt.

There is growing evidence that such abrupt climate change has resulted in the disappearance of human civilizations in the past. About 4,200 years ago, for example, a thriving civilization in Mesopotamia (modern-day Iraq and western Iran) suddenly disappeared. According to researchers, a sudden and widespread drought lasting about two hundred years probably caused the civilization's collapse. Failing agricultural crops were abandoned as people moved to places where they could find food.

If such an abrupt climate change were to occur today in the same region of the world, LDEO researchers say that the effects would reach further than a local drop in agriculture. Due to the current political focus on that particular region, such an event could have globe-spanning consequences.

CFCs gained a lot of attention in the 1980s for their role in damaging the ozone layer. CFCs are synthetic alkanes with chlorine and fluorine attached. They were widely used as refrigerants and propellants (in spray cans) for many decades until scientists realized they were harming the planet's atmosphere and possibly changing its climate.

When CFCs are released into the atmosphere, the chlorine and fluorine atoms readily react with ozone (O_3), a gas that is naturally present. As a result, the ozone molecules are destroyed and are not able to do their job—absorbing harmful ultraviolet light from the sun. This chemical process created the now well-known **ozone hole**, a thinning layer of ozone molecules that is not as efficient at blocking the Sun's harmful rays as it should be. Since the hole was discovered in the 1970s, countries agreed to phase out the production of CFCs on a global scale. However, the "hole," which forms every spring in the Antarctic (September to November), is still increasing in size, covering a larger and larger area.

Global Warming

For decades, scientists and politicians have debated the idea of **global warming**, which proposes that Earth is undergoing an increase in worldwide temperatures. In 2007, the Intergovernmental Panel on Climate Change (IPCC), a worldwide organization that assesses climate change science and risks, said there is a very high likelihood that these recent increases in global temperatures are the result of human activities that add extra carbon dioxide to the atmosphere. The conclusion came from about 600 authors in 40 different countries and was reviewed by more than 100 governments. This review is the most definitive examination of global warming to date.

CARBON DIOXIDE AND CLIMATE CHANGE

Over the past 5 billion years, the temperature of Earth has varied naturally—sometimes the planet has been colder, and sometimes

Figure 7.1　The layers of an ice core can reveal the carbon dioxide present in the atmosphere at different points in time.

it has been warmer. About 10,000 years ago, for example, much of the northern half of Earth was covered by sheets of ice. But this cold period was only one of many in Earth's long history. Throughout Earth's history, the level of carbon dioxide in the atmosphere has fluctuated. When the levels of atmospheric carbon dioxide changed, the temperature of the planet changed as well. Periods with high atmospheric carbon dioxide levels were generally warm, while periods with low atmospheric carbon dioxide levels were generally cold.

One way scientists have learned about the levels of carbon dioxide in the past is through the analysis of ice cores. An **ice core** is a tube of ice, usually drilled out of a glacier or ice sheet, that contains bubbles of air trapped inside layers of snow and ice. Each layer of snow and ice represents roughly a year. The deeper the layer, the older the ice sample. From the size and chemical content of each layer, scientists can draw conclusions about the temperatures at that point in history at that spot on the planet. At the same time, the bubbles of air preserved in each layer contain indicators of the amount of atmospheric carbon dioxide present at that time.

By measuring the carbon dioxide content of the bubbles and comparing it to the known temperatures of the time, scientists have concluded that high levels of atmospheric carbon make for warmer

ALASKA'S RECORD-BREAKING FIRES

Nearly 6 million acres of Alaska's forest and wilderness burned to the ground during the summer of 2004—that's an area about the size of the entire state of Vermont. It was the largest fire in Alaska's state history. Firefighting resources were exhausted, weather conditions were uncooperative, and a lot of people got sick from smoke by simply going outside.

The fires began as soon as the summer started. According to the National Interagency Fire Center, on June 14 and 15 about 17,000 lightning bolts struck the state and started hundreds of fires. These fires, some large and some small, continued to burn and spread over the next three months. By September, about 700 different blazes had been documented.

Despite the near-constant efforts of local and national firefighting teams, the fires didn't really end until the weather changed in the fall. Perhaps not by coincidence, the record-breaking fires were accompanied by record-breaking hot and dry conditions.

Climate experts at the University of Alaska, Fairbanks (UAF) say temperatures across the state were between 3.4° and 5°F (2° and 3°C) warmer than usual, making it the warmest summer on record in many places in the state. At the same time, conditions were unusually dry. Overall, UAF experts estimate the state missed out on about two weeks of rainy days that summer. These unusually warm, dry conditions allowed the fires to spread quickly and easily.

Fortunately, actual flames never reached any major cities in Alaska—but the smoke did. Residents of the second largest city in the state, Fairbanks, reported seeing smoke in the hallways of their homes and offices. At times, there was so much smoke that it blocked out the Sun. State health officials asked people not to go outside. People were not supposed to exercise so as to avoid breathing in extra smoke.

Even today, Fairbanks suffers from carbon-based air pollution created from wildfires. The American Lung Association recently released a report ranking Fairbanks as one of the 25 most polluted metro areas in the nation—

continues

continued

officially coming in at number 21—due largely to wildfire smoke. The ranking officially lumped Fairbanks's air quality among cities such as Detroit, Pittsburgh, Cleveland, and Los Angeles.

Figure 7.2   A fire rages in a forest in Alaska.

temperatures. What is not entirely clear is how much carbon it takes to change the global temperature, how fast global temperatures change as a result of increased atmospheric carbon dioxide levels, and what that really means for humans on Earth.

Carbon Sources

Carbon sources make new forms of carbon or change carbon from one form to another. Stars are the only natural sources of newly created carbon atoms. Usually the specific term "carbon source" refers to a human activity that changes one form of carbon into another, including the burning of fossils fuels by industry and automobiles. Through the process of combustion, the burning of fossil fuels constantly creates new forms of atmospheric carbon. Fossil fuels are made of hydrocarbons. When burned, those hydrocarbons change chemical form and enter the atmosphere as carbon-based gases. In this way, fossil fuel burning becomes a major source of atmospheric carbon.

Industrial burning of fossil fuels in power plants and factories is the largest source of human-created atmospheric carbon. Emissions from automobiles—from simply driving cars—are another major, but much smaller, source. The burning of rain forests in areas around the equator is another major source of carbon dioxide in the atmosphere. (This burning is mostly done to clear land for agriculture.) Altogether, these carbon sources are cause for present and future concerns.

In the United States, the Environmental Protection Agency (EPA) says about 90% of the carbon-based gases released into the atmosphere come from the burning of fossil fuels. Large amounts of these gases have two undesirable effects: First, they increase the amounts of greenhouse gases in the atmosphere (contributing to global warming), and second, they pollute the air near Earth's surface (creating smog). To help control these undesirable effects, both automobile emissions and industrial waste gases are currently regulated by the federal government.

Federal regulation of carbon emissions started with the Clean Air Act in 1963, a national law that regulates the monitoring and measurement of smog and air pollution, and seeks to protect the public from breathing polluted air. The Act was amended in 1966, 1970, 1977, and 1990 to keep up with changes in industry. In the future, it surely will be adjusted again to keep up with changing pollution levels and developments in industry and scientific understanding.

Since the 1970s, the EPA's emissions standards for cars have gotten tougher and have led to new pollution-controlling technologies.

Figure 7.3 These hybrid electric cars are having their batteries charged.

The catalytic converter, new gasoline ingredients, and on-board car computers that monitor engine health and regulate combustion are all examples of new technological developments that have been created to help detect and lower carbon emissions.

One of the latest attempts to reduce carbon emissions in cars is the development of the gasoline-electric hybrid vehicle, or **hybrid car**. A hybrid car uses two sources of energy: a traditional, fossil-fuel-powered engine and a battery that stores electrical energy. A hybrid car can burn fossil fuels and run on a traditional engine or, at other times, the car runs on clean electric power. Because it runs partly on electricity, a hybrid emits much less atmospheric carbon dioxide and other pollutants.

EFFECTS OF GLOBAL WARMING

Scientists agree that the effects of global warming will be widespread. The changes that will occur may be positive in some ways and negative in others. For example, warmer temperatures may allow the planting of new crops in some areas. However, they may also allow the invasion of new insects or even new human diseases in areas where the cold temperature had not allowed the insects or pathogens to live before. Climate changes in some areas may cause conditions to become unsuitable for existing agriculture or certain

THE KYOTO PROTOCOL

Worldwide efforts to reduce carbon emissions officially began in 2005 with the Kyoto Protocol. The Protocol is a United Nations agreement to reduce emissions of carbon dioxide and other greenhouse gases. The role of the United Nations is partially to formulate international laws and security measures. As of November 2007, 174 nations had signed the Kyoto Protocol, thereby committing themselves to reducing carbon emissions on the schedule detailed in the Protocol.

The overall goal is to greatly reduce and then stabilize the production of extra atmospheric carbon, not to stop it completely. To do this, the Protocol sets limits, or caps, on the amounts of greenhouse gases each country can emit. It also allows countries to trade emission credits with each other so if one country is not producing as much carbon as allowed by the Protocol, it can sell its emission credits to another country, which can then produce more than the Protocol allows. The Protocol does not care which country produces what; it only cares about the total amount of carbon pollution produced.

Most developed countries will have to reduce their carbon emissions significantly to meet the emission caps outlined in the Kyoto Protocol. Between 2008 and 2012, on average, the developed countries must reduce emissions by at least 5% below 1990 levels to meet the terms of the agreement. Such a reduction will not be easy to achieve because it could be expensive and because it could require people to make changes in travel, home heating and cooling, and other personal preferences. Whole industries that are major polluters would have to change. Meanwhile, in developing countries that are growing and becoming more prosperous, the demand for power, cars, and polluting industrial processes is increasing, all of which add carbon to the atmosphere.

The United States and China, the countries that rank one and two in carbon emission, have not signed the Kyoto Protocol. In the United States, the Clinton Administration never acted on it, and there were certain terms the Bush Administration did not support. The future of the Kyoto Protocol, like the future of atmospheric carbon, is unclear.

activities. For example, one possibility is that a warmer climate in France will make it unsuitable for growing wine grapes. Another possibility is that glacial melting and lighter snow cover will make Switzerland unsuitable for skiing.

Another problem that may arise with a warming of Earth's surface is a potential rise in sea level caused by melting polar ice. The ice of the Arctic and Antarctic is melting quickly. Glaciers are disappearing at an alarming rate. The resulting melting ice is causing sea levels to rise. There are many heavily populated areas along coastlines that are less than three feet (1 meter) above sea level. By the end of this century, many such areas could be flooded, resulting in tens of millions of people becoming displaced.

Finally, global warming may result in more severe weather phenomena, such as more and stronger hurricanes and tornadoes, more floods in some areas, and more droughts in others. These problems could well affect everyone in one way or another and the rising level of carbon in the atmosphere may be the culprit.

Carbon and Energy

Fossil fuels were formed from the remains of plants and animals that were buried deep underground or underwater. Over long periods of time, pressure and heat converted the remains into coal, oil, and natural gas, which are called fossil fuels.

There are many different types of hydrocarbons, but all of them can burn. When a hydrocarbon burns, its carbon-hydrogen bonds break and release energy in the forms of heat and light. Humans have learned to harness the resulting heat to warm buildings and power engines.

COAL

Coal is an impure rock made of long, branched chains of hydrocarbons. It is often dark and chalky and usually contains small amounts of other elements. Coal's main advantage as an energy resource is its availability. Coal deposits were first discovered near Earth's surface. Because these deposits were easy to reach, coal was one of the first fossil fuels used by humans. Because coal has been used as a fuel for so long, the easily accessed deposits have been stripped, and the coal available now comes from deeper and deeper mines.

In 2002, 5,000 million tons of coal were produced globally. China is the largest coal producer in the world, while the United States is the second largest producer, with widespread coal deposits in the Appalachian Mountains, the western Rockies, and the state of Texas.

The U.S. Department of Energy (DOE) states that about 92% of the coal burned in the United States is used to make electricity, while the rest is used to power industrial plants that make steel, cement, and paper.

Despite its availability and current use, coal is not as widely used today as the other fossil fuels. Coal's major weakness is that it does not burn cleanly. It often contains trace amounts of other elements, including mercury, arsenic, and sulfur, and when it burns, it releases these toxic substances into the air. Over time, coal pollution builds up in the environment. Mercury released during coal combustion, for example, settles in water and builds up in the bodies of fish and shellfish. When these fish and shellfish are eaten by humans and other animals, harmful amounts of mercury can be ingested. In 2008, bluefin tuna served in expensive New York restaurants was found to contain unacceptably high levels of mercury. These fish eat smaller organisms in the ocean, and when these small organisms contain mercury, the toxic element becomes concentrated in the body of the tuna.

The EPA has set tight future limits on mercury emissions from coal-burning industrial plants. As a result, coal is sometimes cleansed of other elements before it is burned to reduce the amount of pollution created. Scientists are currently working on new technologies to prevent the release of harmful substances that arise from coal.

ACID RAIN

One of the problems arising from the burning of "dirty" coal in power plants is acid rain, a condition in which rain, or some other form of precipitation, has a low, strongly acidic pH. Acid rain was first described in the mid-1800s, but did not become a real issue until about 100 years later, when people began to notice areas of dead trees and lakes without any living organisms.

Acid rain occurs when the burning of sulfur-containing coal releases large quantities of sulfur dioxide (SO_2) into the atmosphere. Various nitrogen compounds are also present in the smoke, and they contribute to acid rain, too. In a series of chemical reactions, these substances are converted to sulfuric acid (H_2SO_4) and nitric acid (HNO_3), which are both strong acids. The acids dissolve in water and fall to Earth in rain or in any other form of precipitation. They can also be deposited directly onto the ground, plants, or structures.

The effects of acid rain can be seen in lakes and streams, in forests, and on all kinds of structures. The lowered pH kills fish eggs, fish, and many other organisms that live in lakes and streams. In forests, the acid can kill the leaves and needles of trees. It damages the soil by depleting it of nutrients, which stunts plant growth. Acid rain also eats away at the surfaces of buildings and other structures. Structures made of marble and other calcium-containing stone are particularly sensitive to acid rain.

Acid rain has been reduced with the introduction of technologies that remove the sulfur from the smokestack gases of coal-burning power plants. However, sulfur is present in other fossil fuels, and is introduced into the atmosphere by the exhausts from cars, trucks, and buses. Acid rain is still part of the overall problem of air pollution.

Clean Coal Technology

In recent years, much political and environmental attention has been paid to the idea of "clean coal" technology. Coal is a cheap and relatively available source of energy, but the smoke from its burning creates enormous amounts of air pollution, as well as acid rain.

The concept of "clean coal" is based on the idea that coal can be cleaned of its toxic ingredients by selective burning or washing before it is used as a fuel, thereby reducing the amount of pollutants emitted during combustion. The remaining pollutants can then be collected and stored rather than released into the environment.

If clean coal technology works well enough to be implemented widely in industry, it could have a huge impact on the environment. According to the DOE, the Clean Coal Power Initiative, a plan presented by President George W. Bush in 2001, will help "cut sulfur, nitrogen, and mercury pollutants from power plants by nearly 70% by the year 2018."

The Initiative provides government funding for the creation of new clean coal technologies to help industry reduce coal combustion emissions. At this point, new technologies and programs are still being developed, but it is unclear what will come of the effort. Critics suggest the Initiative is merely a carefully named attempt to keep the coal industry in business, but few environmentalists want to go on record as not supporting the concept of "clean coal." Only the future will tell if clean coal combustion is really possible.

OIL

Oil, or petroleum, is a liquid mixture of medium-length hydrocarbons (shorter than the hydrocarbons in coal, but longer than the hydrocarbons in natural gas). It is usually black or dark brown and has a strong smell, but the characteristics of oil vary greatly, depending on its specific ingredients.

Oil was created by the burial of dead plants and animals under large layers of water and rock. Over millions of years, heat and pressure turned these carbon-based materials into oil.

Oil is extracted from the ground by drilling holes deep into Earth and pumping the oil to the surface. According to the DOE, the world's top five oil-producing nations are Saudi Arabia, Russia, the United States, Iran, and China.

Oil's main advantage as a fossil fuel is its versatility. The DOE states that one 42-gallon barrel of oil actually produces 44 gallons of useable oil products. Like popping popcorn, processing raw oil actually makes it bigger. The processed oil becomes gasoline for cars, diesel fuel for trucks, jet fuel for planes, and heating oil for furnaces. It also is an ingredient in many other petroleum-based products, such as deodorants, ink, crayons, and bubble gum. In the United States, most of the processed oil is used as gasoline.

Oil's main disadvantage is its effect on the surrounding air, land, water, and wildlife. The extraction of oil from the land and the sea can be messy. On land, large, invasive oil drills can disturb local wildlife and destroy landscapes. Oil from broken pipelines sometimes pollutes the land. Much oil drilling takes place in the oceans, where oil spills and leaks can harm or kill ocean life. The process of extracting oil has prompted many political and environmental arguments.

Burning oil, like burning any fossil fuel, releases extra carbon dioxide and other pollutants into the atmosphere. Oil is generally cleaner than coal, but the DOE states that many current environmental laws are aimed at reducing the amount of pollution created by burning oil. Scientists are learning how to remove pollutants from oil before it is burned so that it produces fewer emissions.

NATURAL GAS

Natural gas is a clear, odorless, tasteless gas made of very short and simple hydrocarbons, mostly methane (CH_4). According to the DOE, over half of the homes in the United States are heated with natural gas. Natural gas is also used in homes to fuel stoves, hot water heaters, and clothes dryers. In industry, natural gas is a common raw ingredient in paints, plastics, fertilizers, and medicines. Before natural gas is distributed, a sulfur compound is added to it so that it has a distinct, unpleasant odor. This is a safety precaution intended for the swift detection of leaks, because the gas can be deadly.

The main advantage of natural gas is that it burns cleanly, producing only carbon dioxide and water. Of all the fossil fuels, natural gas is considered the cleanest form of energy. It emits less sulfur, carbon, and nitrogen when burned than coal or oil; and it leaves almost no solid ash particles.

Like oil, natural gas is created when dead plants and animals are buried under layers of water and rock. Over millions of years, heat and pressure turn the carbon-based life forms into natural gas. By studying the surrounding rocks, scientists can locate deposits of natural gas deep underground, but obtaining and storing natural gas is not easy.

To extract natural gas, holes are drilled deep into the Earth and giant pipes are inserted. Once a gas deposit is located, gas flows up the pipeline and is treated at processing plants. Other gases, such as butane and propane, are separated from the methane.

Most of the natural gas that is extracted in the United States is also used there. Natural gas is also imported. The gas is shipped in huge, double-hulled tankers in the form of liquefied natural gas (LNG). Gas to be shipped is cooled to $-260°F$ ($-162°C$), which reduces it to 1/600 of its original volume. At its final destination, the condensed gas is heated, which causes it to expand. It is off-loaded from the tankers into pipelines at off-shore terminals.

Because the demand for natural gas is growing in the United States, there are proposals to build many terminals for LNG tankers. However, because natural gas is highly flammable and explosive, and because the tankers are so large (as long as three football fields), there are many environmental and security issues to be addressed before these terminals are constructed.

CARBON FOOTPRINT

The term "carbon footprint" refers to the impact of human activities on the environment measured in terms of the amounts of greenhouse gases produced. For the most part, the emission of carbon dioxide and other greenhouse gases is associated with the burning of fossil fuels. To simplify matters in discussing carbon footprints, the amounts of the different greenhouse gases produced, such as methane and water vapor, are translated into the equivalent weights of carbon dioxide.

The carbon footprint of one person is a measure of the total amount of greenhouse gases released or produced by that person in the course of one year, directly or indirectly. The footprint includes the amount of carbon dioxide that is emitted as a result of driving and other forms of travel, the amount produced by heating and cooling of the home, and any other activities that directly or indirectly produce greenhouse gases. Carbon dioxide is emitted during the production of the various goods bought in the course of a year. Therefore, these goods also count toward an individual's carbon footprint, as does the amount of electricity a person uses, because fossil fuel probably is burned to generate the electricity.

Another concept arising from the carbon footprint is that of "offsetting." A carbon footprint can be offset by doing something that will remove the carbon dioxide produced from the atmosphere. Such actions include planting trees, or promoting some

TABLE 8.1 **YOUR CARBON FOOTPRINT: AMOUNTS OF CARBON DIOXIDE PRODUCED BY DIFFERENT ACTIVITIES**	
ENERGY USED	**CO_2 PRODUCED**
running computer for 24 hours	1.7 lbs (0.8 kg)
production of 2 plastic bottles	2.2 lbs (1 kg)
production of 5 plastic bags	2.2 lbs (1 kg)
production of 1 cheeseburger	6.8 lbs (3.1 kg)
driving a car 5 miles (8 km)	2.9 lbs (1.3 kg)
taking the bus 5 miles (8 km)	1.8 lbs (0.8 kg)
flying 1,000 miles	1600 lbs (726 kg)
source: http://timeforchange.org/what-is-a-carbon-footprint-definition	

form of clean, renewable energy that will reduce the burning of fossil fuels.

Companies, as well as individuals, have carbon footprints, and the size of these footprints are addressed in the Kyoto Protocol, which regulates greenhouse gas emissions. For countries that have ratified the Protocol, the targets for reducing greenhouse gas emissions are legally binding, but while some aspects of the Protocol are mandatory, others are voluntary. To add flexibility to the requirements, companies can trade rights to greenhouse gas emissions—that is, companies that pollute less can trade unused emission allowances to companies that pollute more. The Protocol also focuses on development of clean technologies that would result in the reduction of some companies' carbon footprints.

FUTURE ENERGY SOURCES

According to the United States Energy Information Administration (EIA) and the book, *Carbon and Its Domestication* (by A.M. Mannion), world energy consumption is increasing quickly. By the year 2025, the EIA predicts that world energy consumption will be more than one and a half times greater than it was in 2001. This estimate is based largely on predictions of growing human populations and their resulting energy needs.

What is not so easy to predict is where all this energy will come from. Fossil fuel supplies are limited, and the atmospheric increases in carbon dioxide caused by their burning are two major problems. Fuel source predictions from the EIA include fossil fuels as the largest source of energy in the future, with nuclear energy and renewable forms of energy at the bottom of the charts.

Nuclear power plants are used to generate electricity. At present there are more than 400 nuclear power plants operating all around the world. About 100 of them are in the United States and 200 are in Europe. The advantage of nuclear power is that no carbon-based pollutants are emitted as with the burning of fossil fuels. However, the disadvantage is that the process produces nuclear wastes. Some of the nuclear wastes decay quickly, in days or months, but some of them take thousands or tens of thousands of years to decay. Highly radioactive pollutants, particularly in the form of spent fuel, must be safely stored for thousands, tens of thousands, or even millions of years. Scientists have been trying for decades to find a safe, stable way to store this material, but so far, no solution has been found. Until questions about the waste storage problem are resolved, use of nuclear energy is unlikely to spread very rapidly. However, there are currently discussions about building new nuclear plants as one way to cut down on the emission of carbon dioxide.

Renewable energy sources include power from solar energy, wind, tides, and waves. Today, these technologies are used on a small scale in some parts of the world. Hydroelectric power, which harnesses the energy of moving water, is the most widely used, and generates about 19% of electricity worldwide. Wind power generates about 1% of the world's total electricity. In some European countries, including Denmark and Spain, it provides a much higher proportion of the electrical needs. Solar power tends to be used in individual homes where it can be used to provide electricity or hot water and heat. Naturally, solar power is more useful in sunny regions, just as wind power is more prevalent in windy areas. In spite of the benefits of these renewable resources, they are not entirely without negatives: Environmental concerns have been raised about the damage caused by the construction of hydroelectric dams, and wind farms pose potential threats to wildlife.

The advantage of renewable energy sources is that they create virtually no pollution and will never run out; the disadvantage is their reliability. Without sun or wind, the device produces no energy. Some sort of backup energy system must be present for a reliable energy supply. As long as humans have obtainable, carbon-based fossil fuels to burn for energy, it seems unlikely another source of energy will ever dominate.

Carbon Products

Many industrial products are carbon-based, including drugs, explosives, and soap. Some of these products are carbon-based polymers, which can be natural or synthetic. Organic polymers consist mainly of long chains of carbon and hydrogen. Other elements, including oxygen, chlorine, nitrogen, and silicon, may be present as well. Organic polymers are formed from the carbon compounds contained in fossil fuels and are used to make the tremendous variety of synthetic products we use everyday. Plastics, drugs, soap, polyester, explosives, and Teflon are some examples of common carbon-based products.

Many commonly used natural and synthetic products are carbon-based polymers. Table 9.1 lists some of them:

TABLE 9.1 ORGANIC AND SYNTHETIC POLYMERS

ORGANIC POLYMERS	MAIN CONSTITUENT
Wool	Protein
Hair	Protein
Fur	Protein
Silk	Protein
Cotton	Carbohydrate
Starch	Carbohydrate
Latex	Alkene
Hemp	Carbohydrate
Flax	Carbohydrate
SYNTHETIC POLYMERS	MAIN CONSTITUENT
Nylon	Amide (nitrogen compound)
Rayon	Carbohydrate
Plastic	Various forms
Neoprene	Alkene
Rubber	Alkene

Source: Mannion, A.M. Carbon and its Domestication. Dordecht, The Netherlands: Springer, 2006., p.47

PLASTICS

Plastics are polymers made from various hydrocarbons found in fossil fuels. Different types of plastics have different ingredients in their polymers, but nearly all of them are chains of carbon atoms bonded to hydrogen and other elements.

Many of the polymers used to make plastics have two unique characteristics: They are transparent and can be melted repeatedly to form new things. The transparency of plastic is important in many products. Food wraps, beverage bottles, headlights, and contact lenses are all made of transparent plastics. The ability of plastics to be melted and shaped into new things makes them suitable for recycling.

Figure 9.1 These products are all made of carbon polymers.

DRUGS

Many drugs are complex carbon-based compounds. Some of these drugs have been discovered in plants, especially in areas of tropical rain forests, where there is enormous plant diversity. These plants sometimes contain unique organic compounds that can be developed into important drugs for treatment of serious diseases, such as cancer. Often, the people who are native to these areas are aware of the medicinal properties of the plants and use them to treat various ailments.

Pharmaceutical companies and researchers looking for new drugs collect plant specimens so that they can analyze them for potentially useful compounds. For example, the western yew tree contains a compound called Taxol that has proven to be an excellent drug for the treatment of various forms of cancer. The potential loss of useful drugs is just one argument against the burning of rain forests to clear land (air pollution and global warming are others).

SOAPS AND DETERGENTS

Soaps and detergents are cleansing agents. Detergents consist of long chains of carbon and hydrogen atoms bonded to an SO_3^- group. Soaps are made from long-chain fatty acids and sodium or some other metal. In the past, the carbon compounds used to make soap were obtained from animal or vegetable fats.

Legend has it that soap was discovered by the ancient Romans while washing their clothes in the river. They noticed that their clothes got cleaner when they were washed in certain areas of the river—primarily areas near a site where animals were sacrificed. Apparently, animal fats from the sacrificed animals washed into the river and accidentally made soapy water that was good for washing clothes.

POLYESTERS

Polyesters are carbon-based polymers that go into an enormous variety of manufactured items. Examples include Dacron and Mylar, as well as plastic bottles and insulating coatings in computers and other electronic equipment. Permanent-press clothing owes its wrinkle-free characteristics to polyester fibers in the fabrics.

Chemically, Dacron and Mylar are polymers made from a ring structure called dimethyl terephthalate and ethylene glycol (HO-CH_2CH_2-OH). The polymer unit is called polyethylene terephthalate, or PET. Dacron fiber is used in tires and fabrics, and is even used to repair blood vessels. Mylar is used in magnetic recording tape. In the 1960s, it was used in huge balloons that were sent into orbit around Earth. Plastic soda containers are made of PET.

NITROGLYCERIN

Nitroglycerin ($C_3H_5N_3O_9$) is a high-energy, highly explosive compound used in dynamite. Each molecule of nitroglycerin contains three carbon atoms bonded to atoms of hydrogen, oxygen, and nitrogen. Alfred Nobel discovered the explosive power of this compound in his laboratory in the 1860s. Unfortunately, his brother and several co-workers were killed accidentally in the process. But with the fortune Nobel made from his explosive discovery, he started the Nobel Prize Foundation.

Nitroglycerin is also widely used in medicine to expand the blood vessels that serve the heart. This relieves the pain of a condition called angina.

TEFLON

Teflon is the brand name for the chemical compound called polytetrafluoroethylene (PTFE). One molecule of PTFE contains two carbon atoms bonded to four fluorine atoms. Many molecules of PTFE can form polymer chains known as fluoropolymers.

Fluoropolymers are able to withstand moderately high temperatures and are one of the slipperiest known solids. As a result, Teflon is commonly used as a nonstick coating, as a shell for bullets, and as an ingredient in waterproof fabrics.

NEW USES OF CARBONS

Scientists continue to explore new forms of carbon for use as raw materials in new products. One of the most interesting fields of research that explores these newly discovered forms is called **nanotechnology**. Nanotechnology is the science and application of very small things, usually less than 0.00004 inches (1 micrometer) in length.

Some scientists are searching for uses of **fullerenes**. Fullerenes are large groups of carbon atoms that are strongly bonded together in very specific, stable shapes. The **buckminsterfullerene**, or **buckyball** for short, is the simplest fullerene and looks like a miniature soccer ball. Buckyballs are made of 60 carbon atoms chemically bonded together. Nanotubes, another form of fullerenes, are cylindrical tubes of carbon atoms bonded together. Nanotubes can be as long as one-tenth of an inch in length. Fullerenes can be synthesized in a chemistry laboratory or found in nature. (Soot contains a lot of buckyballs, for example.)

Until the mid-1980s, no one really knew fullerenes existed. As scientists learn more about these unusual forms of carbon, they realize the fullerenes have a lot of unique properties. They are able

NANO-CHEMICAL KILLERS?

Carbon-based, nano-sized chemicals—substances smaller than three billionths of a foot (one billionth of a meter) in size—are currently being widely studied and used. They have been added to everything from cosmetics to car fluids to "improve" products' performance. But some scientists worry what these new nanoproducts might do to the environment. Because nanoproducts are being added to many products, scientists have begun studying what might happen when they leech out of products and build up in the environment. So far, research results are mixed.

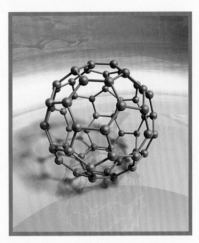

Figure 9.2   A buckyball, also known as a fullerene, is smaller than the average molecule.

Early studies of nanoproducts in the laboratory produced some scary results. In *Scientific American's* "Soil May Counteract Buckyball Danger," author J. R. Minkel reports on one research project that found that buckyballs easily killed populations of bacteria living in laboratory dishes. This result led scientists to wonder whether the small size of buckyballs and other carbon-based nanoproducts made them a danger to living things. The extremely small size, they thought, could allow the nanoproducts to get inside living cells and cause problems.

In another study, researchers added buckyballs to soils containing healthy bacteria. After 180 days, scientists analyzed the soil and found that the buckyballs had had no effect on the soil bacteria. They suspect that the negatively charged buckyballs were attracted to various positively charged material in the soil and did not enter the bacterial cells.

While this recent study produced more comforting research results, it is in no way the end of the story on how nanoproduct pollution could impact the environment and life. Scientists continue to study the effects of carbon-based buckyballs and nanotubes, plus other nanotechnology creations that do not contain carbon.

to withstand high levels of heat and are very strong. Some scientists even speculate that the fullerenes are harder than diamonds.

Because the fullerenes are so heat-resistant, strong, and stable, they could potentially be the raw material for a wide range of products. Fullerene-based armor, medical supplies, computer parts, and even planet-roaming nanorobots are all being considered and researched.

PERIODIC TABLE OF THE ELEMENTS

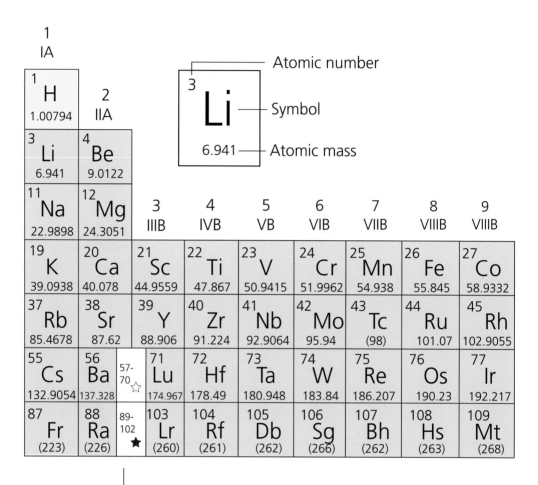

Atomic number

3
Li — Symbol

6.941 — Atomic mass

Numbers in parentheses are atomic mass numbers of most stable isotopes.

								18 VIIIA

Metals

Non-metals

Metalloids

Unknown

			13 IIIA	14 IVA	15 VA	16 VIA	17 VIIA	2 **He** 4.0026
10 VIIIB	11 IB	12 IIB	5 **B** 10.81	6 **C** 12.011	7 **N** 14.0067	8 **O** 15.9994	9 **F** 18.9984	10 **Ne** 20.1798
			13 **Al** 26.9815	14 **Si** 28.0855	15 **P** 30.9738	16 **S** 32.067	17 **Cl** 35.4528	18 **Ar** 39.948
28 **Ni** 58.6934	29 **Cu** 63.546	30 **Zn** 65.409	31 **Ga** 69.723	32 **Ge** 72.61	33 **As** 74.9216	34 **Se** 78.96	35 **Br** 79.904	36 **Kr** 83.798
46 **Pd** 106.42	47 **Ag** 107.8682	48 **Cd** 112.412	49 **In** 114.818	50 **Sn** 118.711	51 **Sb** 121.760	52 **Te** 127.60	53 **I** 126.9045	54 **Xe** 131.29
78 **Pt** 195.08	79 **Au** 196.9655	80 **Hg** 200.59	81 **Tl** 204.3833	82 **Pb** 207.2	83 **Bi** 208.9804	84 **Po** (209)	85 **At** (210)	86 **Rn** (222)
110 **Ds** (271)	111 **Rg** (272)	112 **Uub** (277)	113 **Uut** (284)	114 **Uuq** (285)	115 **Uup** (288)	116 **Uuh** (292)	117 **Uus** ?	118 **Uuo** ?

62 **Sm** 150.36	63 **Eu** 151.966	64 **Gd** 157.25	65 **Tb** 158.9253	66 **Dy** 162.500	67 **Ho** 164.9303	68 **Er** 167.26	69 **Tm** 168.9342	70 **Yb** 173.04
94 **Pu** (244)	95 **Am** 243	96 **Cm** (247)	97 **Bk** (247)	98 **Cf** (251)	99 **Es** (252)	100 **Fm** (257)	101 **Md** (258)	102 **No** (259)

ELECTRON CONFIGURATIONS

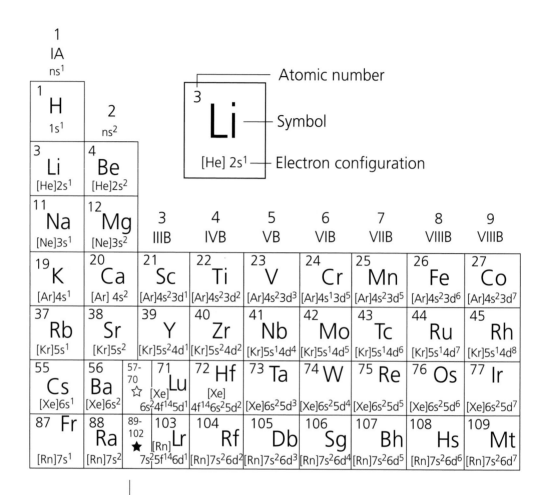

									18
									VIIIA
									ns^2np^6

			13	14	15	16	17		2 He
			IIIA	IVA	VA	VIA	VIIA		$1s^2$
			ns^2np^1	ns^2np^2	ns^2np^3	ns^2np^4	ns^2np^5		

			5 B	6 C	7 N	8 O	9 F	10 Ne
			$[He]2s^22p^1$	$[He]2s^22p^2$	$[He]2s^22p^3$	$[He]2s^22p^4$	$[He]2s^22p^5$	$[He]2s^22p^6$

10	11	12	13 Al	14 Si	15 P	16 S	17 Cl	18 Ar
VIIIB	IB	IIB	$[Ne]3s^23p^1$	$[Ne]3s^23p^2$	$[Ne]3s^23p^3$	$[Ne]3s^23p^4$	$[Ne]3s^23p^5$	$[Ne]3s^23p^6$

28 Ni	29 Cu	30 Zn	31 Ga	32 Ge	33 As	34 Se	35 Br	36 Kr
$[Ar]4s^23d^8$	$[Ar]4s^13d^{10}$	$[Ar]4s^23d^{10}$	$[Ar]4s^24p^1$	$[Ar]4s^24p^2$	$[Ar]4s^24p^3$	$[Ar]4s^24p^4$	$[Ar]4s^24p^5$	$[Ar]4s^24p^6$
46 Pd	47 Ag	48 Cd	49 In	50 Sn	51 Sb	52 Te	53 I	54 Xe
$[Kr]4d^{10}$	$[Kr]5s^14d^{10}$	$[Kr]5s^24d^{10}$	$[Kr]5s^25p^1$	$[Kr]5s^25p^2$	$[Kr]5s^25p^3$	$[Kr]5s^25p^4$	$[Kr]5s^25p^5$	$[Kr]5s^25p^6$
78 Pt	79 Au	80 Hg	81 Tl	82 Pb	83 Bi	84 Po	85 At	86 Rn
$[Xe]6s^15d^9$	$[Xe]6s^15d^{10}$	$[Xe]6s^25d^{10}$	$[Xe]6s^26p^1$	$[Xe]6s^26p^2$	$[Xe]6s^26p^3$	$[Xe]6s^26p^4$	$[Xe]6s^26p^5$	$[Xe]6s^26p^6$
110 Ds	111 Rg	112 Uub	113 Uut	114 Uuq	115 Uup	116 Uuh	117 Uus	118 Uuo
$[Rn]7s^16d^9$	$[Rn]7s^16d^{10}$	$[Rn]7s^26d^{10}$	?	?	?	?	?	?

62 Sm	63 Eu	64 Gd	65 Tb	66 Dy	67 Ho	68 Er	69 Tm	70 Yb
[Xe]	[Xe]	[Xe]	[Xe]	[Xe]	[Xe]	[Xe]	[Xe]	[Xe]
$6s^24f^65d^0$	$6s^24f^75d^0$	$6s^24f^75d^1$	$6s^24f^95d^0$	$6s^24f^{10}5d^0$	$6s^24f^{11}5d^0$	$6s^24f^{12}5d^0$	$6s^24f^{13}5d^0$	$6s^24f^{14}5d^0$
94 Pu	95 Am	96 Cm	97 Bk	98 Cf	99 Es	100 Fm	101 Md	102 No
[Rn]	[Rn]	[Rn]	[Rn]	[Rn]	[Rn]	[Rn]	[Rn]	[Rn]
$7s^25f^66d^0$	$7s^25f^76d^0$	$7s^25f^76d^1$	$7s^25f^96d^0$	$7s^25f^{10}6d^0$	$7s^25f^{11}6d^0$	$7s^25f^{12}6d^0$	$7s^25f^{13}6d^0$	$7s^25f^{14}6d^1$

TABLE OF ATOMIC MASSES

ELEMENT	SYMBOL	ATOMIC NUMBER	ATOMIC MASS	ELEMENT	SYMBOL	ATOMIC NUMBER	ATOMIC MASS
Actinium	Ac	89	(227)	Francium	Fr	87	(223)
Aluminum	Al	13	26.9815	Gadolinium	Gd	64	157.25
Americium	Am	95	243	Gallium	Ga	31	69.723
Antimony	Sb	51	121.76	Germanium	Ge	32	72.61
Argon	Ar	18	39.948	Gold	Au	79	196.9655
Arsenic	As	33	74.9216	Hafnium	Hf	72	178.49
Astatine	At	85	(210)	Hassium	Hs	108	(263)
Barium	Ba	56	137.328	Helium	He	2	4.0026
Berkelium	Bk	97	(247)	Holmium	Ho	67	164.9303
Beryllium	Be	4	9.0122	Hydrogen	H	1	1.00794
Bismuth	Bi	83	208.9804	Indium	In	49	114.818
Bohrium	Bh	107	(262)	Iodine	I	53	126.9045
Boron	B	5	10.81	Iridium	Ir	77	192.217
Bromine	Br	35	79.904	Iron	Fe	26	55.845
Cadmium	Cd	48	112.412	Krypton	Kr	36	83.798
Calcium	Ca	20	40.078	Lanthanum	La	57	138.9055
Californium	Cf	98	(251)	Lawrencium	Lr	103	(260)
Carbon	C	6	12.011	Lead	Pb	82	207.2
Cerium	Ce	58	140.115	Lithium	Li	3	6.941
Cesium	Cs	55	132.9054	Lutetium	Lu	71	174.967
Chlorine	Cl	17	35.4528	Magnesium	Mg	12	24.3051
Chromium	Cr	24	51.9962	Manganese	Mn	25	54.938
Cobalt	Co	27	58.9332	Meitnerium	Mt	109	(268)
Copper	Cu	29	63.546	Mendelevium	Md	101	(258)
Curium	Cm	96	(247)	Mercury	Hg	80	200.59
Darmstadtium	Ds	110	(271)	Molybdenum	Mo	42	95.94
Dubnium	Db	105	(262)	Neodymium	Nd	60	144.24
Dysprosium	Dy	66	162.5	Neon	Ne	10	20.1798
Einsteinium	Es	99	(252)	Neptunium	Np	93	(237)
Erbium	Er	68	167.26	Nickel	Ni	28	58.6934
Europium	Eu	63	151.966	Niobium	Nb	41	92.9064
Fermium	Fm	100	(257)	Nitrogen	N	7	14.0067
Fluorine	F	9	18.9984	Nobelium	No	102	(259)

ELEMENT	SYMBOL	ATOMIC NUMBER	ATOMIC MASS	ELEMENT	SYMBOL	ATOMIC NUMBER	ATOMIC MASS
Osmium	Os	76	190.23	Silicon	Si	14	28.0855
Oxygen	O	8	15.9994	Silver	Ag	47	107.8682
Palladium	Pd	46	106.42	Sodium	Na	11	22.9898
Phosphorus	P	15	30.9738	Strontium	Sr	38	87.62
Platinum	Pt	78	195.08	Sulfur	S	16	32.067
Plutonium	Pu	94	(244)	Tantalum	Ta	73	180.948
Polonium	Po	84	(209)	Technetium	Tc	43	(98)
Potassium	K	19	39.0938	Tellurium	Te	52	127.6
Praseodymium	Pr	59	140.908	Terbium	Tb	65	158.9253
Promethium	Pm	61	(145)	Thallium	Tl	81	204.3833
Protactinium	Pa	91	231.036	Thorium	Th	90	232.0381
Radium	Ra	88	(226)	Thulium	Tm	69	168.9342
Radon	Rn	86	(222)	Tin	Sn	50	118.711
Rhenium	Re	75	186.207	Titanium	Ti	22	47.867
Rhodium	Rh	45	102.9055	Tungsten	W	74	183.84
Roentgenium	Rg	111	(272)	Ununbium	Uub	112	(277)
Rubidium	Rb	37	85.4678	Uranium	U	92	238.0289
Ruthenium	Ru	44	101.07	Vanadium	V	23	50.9415
Rutherfordium	Rf	104	(261)	Xenon	Xe	54	131.29
Samarium	Sm	62	150.36	Ytterbium	Yb	70	173.04
Scandium	Sc	21	44.9559	Yttrium	Y	39	88.906
Seaborgium	Sg	106	(266)	Zinc	Zn	30	65.409
Selenium	Se	34	78.96	Zirconium	Zr	40	91.224

GLOSSARY

Acid rain   Rain or any other form of precipitation that is strongly acidic due to sulfur and nitrogen compounds released through the burning of fossil fuels, particularly coal.

Addition reaction   Reaction in which atoms are added to reactants, often at carbon-carbon double or triple bonds.

Alcohol   A compound containing an OH group.

Alkane   A hydrocarbon compound containing only single bonds.

Alkene   A hydrocarbon compound containing one or more double bonds.

Alkyne   A hydrocarbon compound containing one or more triple bonds.

Allotropes   The naturally occurring different physical forms of an element.

Amines   The functional group NH_2.

Amino acids   The building blocks of proteins;

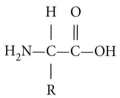

Aromatic compounds   Compounds in which the carbon atoms form a ring, which contains double bonds.

Atmosphere   The layer of gases surrounding the planet and held in place by gravity.

Atoms   The building blocks of all matter; the smallest unit of an element that has the characteristics of the element.

Atomic mass   The total number of protons and neutrons in the nucleus of an atom; also called atomic weight.

Atomic number   The number of protons in the nucleus of an atom.

Atomic weight   The total number of protons and neutrons in the nucleus of an atom; also called atomic mass.

Biomolecules   Molecules found in living things.

Biosphere   The part of Earth that contains living things; includes all inhabitable parts of the atmosphere, oceans, and land.

Buckminsterfullerene, or buckyball   The simplest form of a fullerene; resembles a miniature soccer ball; made of 60 carbon atoms stuck together.

Carbohydrates   Large class of biomolecules that includes a wide variety of compounds, including sugars, starch, cellulose, and glycogen.

Carbon   The nonmetallic element with atomic number 6; essential element for life on Earth.

Carbon chemistry   Organic chemistry.

Carbon cycle   The cyclic movement of carbon through Earth, atmosphere, land, oceans, and living things.

Carbon dating   A process that uses the relative abundance of the radioactive isotope carbon-14 to determine the age of the remains or products of living things; can be used for materials up to about 60,000 years old.

Carbon sink   A place where carbon is stored for long periods of time; the oceans are one example of a carbon sink.

Carbon source   Something that makes new forms of carbon.

Carbonyl group   Consists of a carbon atom double bonded to an oxygen atom; found in different types of functional groups.

Carboxyl group   A functional group (COOH) found in organic acids (carboxylic acids) and in amino acids.

Chemical bond   An attraction between atoms involving the sharing, loss, or gain of electrons; holds the atoms of a compound together.

Chemical equation   A shorthand representation showing the reactants and products of a chemical reaction and their relative quantities.

Chemical reaction The process in which one or more chemical substances are changed into other substances.

Chemical properties The properties that determine whether a substance can undergo particular chemical reactions and under what conditions.

Chemical symbol A unique one- or two-letter symbol assigned to each of the elements.

Chlorofluorocarbons (CFCs) Carbon compounds that contain chlorine and fluorine and that react with and destroy the ozone layer in the atmosphere.

Climate Long-term patterns of weather.

Compound A substance formed by the chemical combination of atoms of two or more elements.

Decay The process in which the nucleus of a radioactive atom gives off energy and/or particles to produce an atom of a different element.

Decomposer Bacteria, fungi, and other soil organisms that break down the remains of dead organisms, returning carbon and other elements to the environment.

Decomposition Decay; the breakdown of the remains of dead organisms.

Digestion The breakdown of food into small molecules that can enter the cells of the body.

Deoxyribonucleic acid (DNA) A polymer of nucleotides that contains the hereditary information of the organism.

Double bond A bond formed by the sharing of two pairs of electrons between two atoms.

Electrons Negatively charged particles found in the space around the nucleus of an atom.

Element One of a class of substances that cannot be broken down to a simpler substance by normal chemical means.

Elimination reaction   Reaction in which atoms are eliminated from adjacent carbon atoms producing a double bond between the carbons.

Ester   A function group.

$$R - \overset{\overset{\displaystyle O}{\|}}{C} - OR$$

Fats   Substances made from glycerol and fatty acids; includes animal fats, which are solid, and vegetable oils, which are liquid.

Fossil fuels   Coal, oil, and natural gas; all formed from the remains of plants and animals under great heat and pressure over long periods of time.

Fuel   Anything that burns.

Fullerene   An allotrope of carbon; consists of carbon atoms joined together in spheres or tubes.

Functional group   Atoms or a group of atoms that give certain molecules their characteristic properties.

Genes   units of genetic material that carry information for the production of proteins.

Genetic code   The hereditary information passed from generation to generation and found in the order of nitrogen bases in DNA; the code controls protein synthesis in the organism.

Gigaton (Gt)   A unit equal to one billion metric tons; often used to measure carbon and carbon dioxide in the Earth.

Global warming   An increase in worldwide temperatures at the surface of Earth.

Greenhouse gases   Gases responsible for the greenhouse effect, including carbon dioxide, methane, and water vapor, among others. The greenhouse effect is the effect of gases in the atmosphere that trap heat near the surface of Earth, causing warming surface temperatures.

Half-life   The time in which half the atoms in a radioactive sample undergo decay.

Hybrid car   A car that uses two sources of energy: a traditional, fossil-fuel powered engine plus a battery that stores electric energy.

Hydrocarbon   Any compound that consists only of carbon and hydrogen atoms.

Ice age   A period in Earth's history where much of the planet was covered in ice.

Ice core   A tube of ice, usually drilled out of a glacier or ice sheet; often used in climate research.

Inorganic carbon   Carbon that does not come from living things.

Inorganic chemistry   The chemistry of substances and compounds from nonliving matter, such as rocks and minerals.

Interglacial period   A period between ice ages when Earth is relatively warm.

Ion   An atom that has lost or gained one or more electrons so that is has an electrical charge.

Isotopes   Atoms of an element that differ in the number of neutrons in the nucleus.

Lipids   Class of biomolecules that includes fats and oils; all lipids are insoluble in water and similar substances.

Molecule   The smallest unit of a compound that has the same chemical constituents as the compound in the same proportions.

Nanotechnology   A field of science that focuses on very small things; usually less than 0.00004 inches (1 micrometer) in length.

Neutrons   Electrically neutral particles found in the nucleus of an atom.

Nonmetal   An element that displays certain properties, including being a poor conductor of electricity, dull appearance, brittle, and typically having relatively low melting and boiling points.

Nucleic acids DNA and RNA; DNA carries the hereditary information, while RNA carries this information from the cell nucleus to the sites of protein synthesis.

Nucleotides The building blocks of DNA. Each nucleotide is made of a phosphate, a sugar, and a nitrogenous base.

Nucleus The dense central portion of an atom that contains protons and neutrons; the control center of the cell; contains the DNA.

Organic chemistry The chemistry of carbon and its compounds.

Ozone hole A diminished layer of O_3 molecules in the atmosphere that is not as efficient at blocking the Sun's harmful rays as it should be.

Periodic table A chart of all the elements organized in order of increasing atomic number and characteristics.

pH A measure of acidity—the hydrogen ion concentration.

Photosynthesis The process by which chlorophyll-containing plants and other organisms use carbon dioxide, water, and energy from sunlight to synthesize carbohydrates; oxygen is given off as a by-product.

Physical properties The properties of a substance that can be directly observed or measured without a chemical change.

Plastics Polymers made by heating various hydrocarbons.

Polyesters Fibers made from specific types of carbon-based polymers.

Polymer A chain of repeating small units bonded together.

Product New substance(s) created by a chemical reaction.

Proteins A large class of biomolecules made up of amino acids; enzymes and many hormones are proteins, as are parts of the skin, hair, nails.

Protons The positively charged particles inside the nucleus of an atom.

Reactant The substance(s) at the start of a chemical reaction.

Renewable energy source   Source of energy, such as wind, waves, tidal, or solar, that does not deplete any resource; renewable energy sources are also nonpolluting.

Respiration   The process by which organisms break down nutrients for energy; oxygen is needed for the reactions, and carbon dioxide and water are produced.

Ribonucleic acid (RNA)   A molecule found within cells that carries information to make proteins from DNA to other cell parts.

Single bond   A bond formed by the sharing of one pair of electrons by two atoms.

Substitution reaction   A reaction in which two reactants exchange parts, forming a new substance.

Teflon   The brand name for the chemical compound called polytetrafluoroethylene, or PTFE.

Triple bond   The sharing of three pairs of electrons by two atoms.

Weather   The rapidly changing conditions at Earth's surface, including temperature, precipitation, cloud cover, and wind.

Weathering   The breakdown of rocks on the surface of Earth by the action of wind, water, and chemicals.

BIBLIOGRAPHY

"2004 Wildland Fire Season Summary." Division of Air Quality: Air Monitoring and Quality Assurance. State of Alaska Department of Conservation Web site. Available online. URL: http://www.dec.state.ak.us/air/am/2004_wf_sum.htm.

"Abrupt Climate Change." Lamont-Doherty Earth Observatory, Columbia University Web site. Available online. URL: http://www.ldeo.columbia.edu/res/div/ocp/arch/.

"Anchorage, Fairbanks at Opposite Ends of Air Quality Report." The KTVA Channel 11 Web site. May 4, 2007. Available online. URL: http://www.ktva.com/alaska/ci_5819495.

"The Carbon Cycle." National Aeronautics and Space Administration Web site. Available online. URL: http://eobglossary.gsfc.nasa.gov//Library/CarbonCycle/carbon_cycle.html.

"Clean Coal Technology & The President's Clean Coal Power Initiative." U.S. Department of Energy Web site. Available online. URL: http://www.fossil.energy.gov/programs/powersystems/cleancoal/.

"Climate Change 2007: The Physical Science Basis." Intergovernmental Panel on Climate Change Web site. Available online. URL: http://www.ipcc.ch/SPM2feb07.pdf.

Cottrell, William H. *The Book of Fire*. Missoula, Mont.: Mountain Press Publishing Company (in cooperation with the National Park Foundation), 2004.

"Could Life Be Based on Silicon Rather than Carbon?" NASA Astrobiology Institute Web site. Available online. URL: http://nai.arc.nasa.gov/astrobio/feat_questions/silicon_life.cfm.

"The Global Carbon Cycle." Lamont Doherty Earth Observatory, Columbia University Web Site. Available online. URL: http://www.ldeo.columbia.edu/edu/dees/V1003/lectures/global_carbon_cycle/index.html.

Guch, Ian. *The Complete Idiot's Guide to Chemistry*. New York: Alpha Books, 2003.

"Highlights for the 2004 Wildland Fire Season," National Interagency Fire Center Web site. Available online. URL: http://www.nifc.gov/stats/summaries/summary_2004.html.

"History of Carbon." University of Kentucky: Center for Applied Energy Research Web site. Available online. URL: http://www.caer.uky.edu/carbon/history/carbonhistory.shtml.

Mannion, A.M. *Carbon and its Domestication.* Dordrecht, The Netherlands: Springer, 2006.

Moore, John T. *Chemistry Made Simple.* New York: Broadway Books, 2004.

Minkel, J.R. "Soil May Counteract Buckyball Danger." *Scientific American* Web site. March 27, 2007. Available online. URL: http://www.sciam.com/article.cfm?articleID=95B9953F-E7F2-99DF-35573AC932414FF1&sc=I100322.

"The Nature of Diamonds." The American Museum of Natural History Web site. Available online. URL: http://www.amnh.org/exhibitions/diamonds.

"NASA's Oceanography." National Aeronautics and Space Administration Web site. Available online. URL: http://science.hq.nasa.gov/oceans/system/carbon.html.

"The Ocean and the Carbon Cycle." National Aeronautics and Space Administration Oceanography Web site. Available online. URL: http://science.hq.nasa.gov/oceans/system/carbon.html.

"Picking a Winner in Clean-Coal Technology." MIT Technology Review Web site. Available online. URL: http://www.technologyreview.com/Energy/18398.

"Wildland Fire Statistics." National Interagency Fire Center Web site. Available online. URL: http://www.nifc.gov/stats/historicalstats.html.

Winter, Arthur. *Organic Chemistry for Dummies.* Hoboken, N.J.: Wiley Publishing, 2005.

Worldwatch Institute. *Vital Signs 2007-2008.* New York: W.W. Norton, 2007.

FURTHER READING

Brezina, Corona. *Cutting Edge Careers: Careers in Nanotechnology.* New York: Rosen Publishing Group, 2007.

Cottrell, William H. *The Book of Fire.* Missoula, Mont.: Mountain Press Publishing Company (in cooperation with the National Park Foundation), 2004.

Harmon, Daniel E. *Your Government—How It Works: The Environmental Protection Agency.* New York: Chelsea House Publishing, 2002.

Hopkins, William G. *The Green World: Photosynthesis and Respiration.* New York: Chelsea House Publishing, 2006.

Saucerman, Linda. *Understanding the Elements of the Periodic Table: Carbon.* New York: Rosen Central, 2005.

Saunders, Nigel and Steven Chapman. *Energy Essentials: Fossil Fuel.* Chicago: Raintree Publishers, 2005.

Slade, Suzanne. *The Carbon Cycle.* New York: PowerKids Press, 2007.

Snedden, Robert. *Essential Energy: Energy Alternatives.* Chicago: Heinemann Publishing, 2006.

Tanaka, Shelley. *Climate Change.* Toronto: Groundwood Books, 2004.

Web Sites

The Carbon Cycle
National Aeronautics and Space Administration (NASA)

http://Earthobservatory.nasa.gov/Library/CarbonCycle/.

NASA's description of the planet's carbon cycle and current research.

Department of Energy Kid's Pages

http://eia.doe.gov

Coal Page: http://www.eia.doe.gov/kids/energyfacts/sources/non-renewable/coal.html

Natural Gas Page: http://www.eia.doe.gov/kids/energyfacts/
sources/non-renewable/naturalgas.html
Petroleum Page: http://www.eia.doe.gov/kids/energyfacts/
sources/non-renewable/oil.html

The United States Department of Energy tells how coal, natural gas, and petroleum are formed, obtained, and used in this country.

International Panel on Climate Change
http://www.ipcc.ch/

The IPCC's job is to keep an eye on climate change research. They read and try to make sense of all the scientific papers on global warming. Although some of the information on this Web site is tough and technical, it is a good place to start for a scientific, unbiased, global look at climate change.

It's Elemental: Carbon
The Jefferson Lab at the Thomas Jefferson National Accelerator Facility
http://education.jlab.org/itselemental/ele006.html

Carbon basics and information from the periodic table. A good source for a school report on the element carbon.

Missoula Fire Sciences Lab
United States Forest Service
http://www.firelab.org/

Researchers at the Firelab study the behavior, chemistry, and fuels of forest fires. Browse this site to learn more about forest fire science and current research projects.

The Nature of Diamonds
American Museum of Natural History
http://www.amnh.org/exhibitions/diamonds/

Learn about the history, chemistry, and industry of diamonds— the hardest form of carbon on Earth—by exploring these Web pages from a former exhibit at the American Museum of Natural History.

TryScience!

New York Hall of Science

http://www.tryscience.org/

Science experiments, online field trips, and links to science and technology centers worldwide. Explore the Earth Science and Biological Sciences experiments to learn more about carbon chemistry.

PHOTO CREDITS

INDEX

A

acetylene, 28, 29
acidity, oceans and, 48
acid rain, 77
addition reactions, 33
adenine, 40–41
agriculture, global warming and, 72–74
Alaska, 69–70
alchemy, 12
alcohols, 30
algae, 49, 54
alkanes, 24–26
alkenes, 26–28
alkynes, 28–29
allotropes, 18
amine groups, 32, 36
amino acids, 31, 35–36, 60
ammonia, 32
angina, 88
Antarctic ozone hole, 66
antifreeze, 27
Appalachian Mountains, 76
appearance, 19
argon, atmosphere and, 60
aromatic hydrocarbons, 29–30
atmosphere, 47, 59–62. *See also* greenhouse gases
atomic mass, 9, 12, 19
atomic number, 9, 12, 19
atomic weight, 9, 12, 19
atoms, 7–8
ATP (adenosine triphosphate), respiration and, 44
automobiles, 6, 71–72

B

benzene rings, 29
bicarbonate, oceans and, 48
biomolecules
  carbohydrates, 37–38, 44
  lipids, 39
  nucleic acids, 39–41
  overview of, 35
  proteins, 35–37
biosphere, 42–43
birth control pills, 28–29
boiling points, 19
bonds, chemical, 20–22, 36–37
Boyle, Robert, 8
Bronze Age, 4
buckminsterfullerenes, 88–90
buckyballs, 88–90
Bush, George W., 78
butane, 25

C

calcium carbonate, 50
carbohydrates, 37–38, 44
carbon-12, 10–11, 12
carbon-13, 10–11
carbon-14, 10–11
Carbon and Its Domestication (Mannion), 82
carbon cycle
  atmosphere and, 47
  carbon sinks and, 49, 50, 53–54
  coal and, 46
  decomposition, fossil fuel formation and, 46, 51
  land and, 50–53
  living organisms and, 53
  oceans and, 47–50
  oil, natural gas and, 47
  overview of, 42–44, 55–56
  photosynthesis and, 44, 56
  respiration and, 44, 56
  weathering and, 45, 52
carbon dating, 10–11
carbon dioxide
  atmosphere and, 60–62
  climate change and, 67–70
  decomposition and, 46
  fires and, 48
  formula of, 23
  as greenhouse gas, 64–65

carbon dioxide *(continued)*
   ice ages and, 62–63
   oceans and, 47–50
   photosynthesis and, 44
   weathering and, 45
carbon emissions, 51, 71–72, 73,
   81–82
carbon footprints, 80–82
carbon fuels. *See* fuels
carbon monoxide, 65
carbon reservoirs, 42, 52
carbon sinks, 49, 50, 53–54
carbonyl groups, 31
carboxyl groups, 31, 36
carboxylic acid, 31
catalytic converters, 72
cellulose, 37–38
CFCs (chlorofluorocarbons),
   64–65
chalk, 23
charcoal, 3–4, 16–17
chemical bonds, 20–22, 36–37
chemical formulas, 9
chemical properties of carbon,
   20–21
chemical reactions
   addition, 33
   elimination, 33
   overview of, 32–33
   substitution, 33
chemical symbols, 9
China, 73, 76, 79
chlorofluorocarbons (CFCs),
   64–65
chlorophyll, photosynthesis
   and, 44
chromatin, 40
chromosomes, 40
Clean Air Acts, 71
Clean Coal Power Initiative, 78
climate
   carbon dioxide and, 64–65,
     67–70
   greenhouse gases and, 64–66

overview of, 62
past, 62–63
present, 63
coal, 3–4, 17, 46, 75–78
coke, 4
combustion engines, 71
compounds, 12–13
conductivity, 19
creation of carbon, 16–17
cytosine, 40–41

D

Dacron, 87
Davy, Humphrey, 17–18
decomposition, 46, 51
deforestation, 48, 71
Denmark, 83
deoxyribose, 40
detergents, 86–87
diabetes, 38
diamonds, 1, 17, 19, 22
dipeptides, 36–37
disaccharides, 38
DNA (deoxyribonucleic acid),
   39–41
double bonds, 21–22, 39
drought, 74
drugs, 86
dynamite, 87–88

E

electrons, 7–8, 14, 20–22
elements, 8, 9, 13–15
elimination reactions, 33
emissions, 51, 71–72, 73,
   81–82
energy, 80–83. *See also* fuels
enzymes, 35
esters, 31
ethane, 30, 34
ethyl alcohol, 30, 33
ethylene, 26–27, 33–34
ethylene glycol, 27
ethynyl estradiol, 28–29

F

Fairbanks, Alaska, 69–70
fats, 39
fatty acids, 39, 86–87
fires, 48, 67–70, 71
flooding, 74
fluoropolymers, 88
forests, 48, 54, 71
forms of carbon, 17–18
fossil fuels
    carbon cycle and, 46
    coal and, 3–4, 17, 46, 75–78
    global warming and, 71
    natural gas, 6, 23, 26, 29, 47,
        79–80
    oil, 4–6, 47, 78–79
fragrances, 29, 31
fuels
    coal and, 3–4, 17, 46,
        75–78
    future sources of, 82–83
    global warming and, 1–2
    history of, 2–3
    natural gas, 6, 23, 26, 29, 47,
        79–80
    oil, 4–6, 47, 78–79
fullerenes, 18, 88–90
functional groups, 30

G

gas. *See* natural gas
genes, 40
genetic code, 40–41
gigatons, defined, 43
glaciers, 74
global warming. *See also*
    greenhouse gases
    carbon dioxide and, 64–65,
        67–70
    carbon sources and, 70–72
    effects of, 72–74
    Kyoto Protocol and, 73, 82
glucose, 38
glycerol, 39

glycogen, 37
graphite, 1, 17–18, 19, 22
greenhouse gases. *See also* global
    warming
        carbon footprints and,
            80–82
        climate and, 64–66
        Kyoto Protocol and, 73
groups, periodic table and,
    13–14
guanine, 40–41

H

half-lives, 10
handedness, 37, 57–58
hardness, 19
helium, 16–17
helix structure, 37
history of carbon use, 2–3, 5
hormones, 27, 28–29
Horta, 57
hurricanes, 74
hybrid vehicles, 72
hydrocarbons
    alkanes, 24–26
    alkenes, 26–28
    alkynes, 28–29
    aromatic, 29–30
    coal and, 75
    fossil fuels and, 71
    natural gas and, 79
    oil and, 78
    plastics and, 85

I

ice ages, 63
ice cores, 68–70
ice sheets, 63, 74
Industrial Revolution, 4
inorganic carbon, oceans and,
    47–48
inorganic chemistry, 2
insulin, 38
interglacial periods, 63

ions, 8
Iron Age, 4
isotopes, 9, 10–11

K
Kennewick Man, 11
kerosene, 6
Kyoto Protocol, 73, 82

L
Lamont-Doherty Earth
   Observatory (LDEO), 65
land, carbon cycle and,
   50–53
left-handedness, 37, 57–58
lignite, 46
limestone, 50
lipids, 39
liquified natural gas (LNG), 80
living organisms, 53, 55–56

M
melting points, 19
memorial diamonds, 22
Mendeleyev, Dmitri, 13
mercury, 76, 78
Mesopotamia, 65
metabolism, respiration
   and, 44
methane, 24–26, 64, 65, 79
mining, 52–53
Minkel, J.R., 89
molecules, 13
monosaccharides, 38, 40
Mylar, 87

N
naming of carbon compounds,
   23–24
nanotechnology, 88–90
natural gas
   acetylene and, 29
   alkanes and, 26

carbon cycle and, 47
formula of, 23
history of, 6
overview of, 79–80
neutrons, 7–8, 9
nitric acid, 77
nitrogen, atmosphere and, 60
nitroglycerin, 87–88
nitrous oxide, 64
Nobel, Alfred, 87–88
nonmetals, 19
nuclear power plants, 82–83
nuclei, 7
nucleic acids, 39–41
nucleosynthesis, 16–17
nucleotides, 40

O
oceans, 47–50, 54, 74
offsets, carbon dioxide and,
   81–82
oil, 47, 78–79
organic chemistry, 2
oxygen
   algae and, 49
   atmosphere and, 60–62
   coal formation and, 46
   decomposition and, 46, 47
   respiration and, 44
ozone, 64–66
ozone hole, 66

P
pancreas, 38
peat, 46
pencils. *See* graphite
peptide bonds, 36–37
periodic table of the elements,
   13–15
periods, periodic table and,
   13–14
petroleum, 47, 78–79
pH, 48. *See also* acid rain

phosphates, 40
photosynthesis
    atmosphere and, 60–61
    carbon cycle and, 44, 49–50,
        54, 56
physical properties of carbon,
    18–19
plants, 44, 46, 60–61
plastics, 26–27, 85
polyesters, 87
polyethylene, 26–27, 87
polymers
    carbon products of, 84–85
    overview of, 27–28
    polyesters and, 87
    soaps and, 86–87
    Teflon and, 88
polypeptides, 37
polypropylene, 27
polysaccharides, 38
polytetrafluoroethylene
    (PTFE), 88
prefixes, nomenclature and,
    23–24
products, defined, 32
propane, 25
propylene, 27
proteins, 35–37, 60
protons, 7–8, 9, 16–17

R
radioactive decay, 10–11
rain forests, 71
reactants, 32
reactions, chemical
    addition, 33
    elimination, 33
    overview of, 32–33
    substitution, 33
recycling, 85
reforestation, 54
renewable energy sources, 83
replication, 40–41

reservoirs, carbon, 42, 52
respiration, 44, 56, 60–61
right-handedness, 37, 57–58
ripening, hormones and, 27
RNA (ribonucleic acid), 39–41
rocks, carbon cycle and, 45,
    50–53

S
saturated fats, 39
science fiction, 57–58
sea levels, 74
sediments, 50
series, 19
shells, 20
silicon-based life forms,
    57–58
single bonds, 21
sinks, carbon, 49, 50, 53–54
smoke, 48, 69
soaps, 86–87
solar power, 83
solar system, 16–17
solubility, 39
Spain, 83
starches, 37–38
stars, 16–17, 70–71
Star Trek, 57
steam engines, 4
steel, 4
substitution reactions, 33
suffixes, nomenclature and,
    23–24
sugar (table), 23
sugars, 37–38
sulfur dioxide, 77
synthetic diamonds, 22
synthetic polymers, 85

T
Taxol, 86
Teflon, 88
thymine, 40–41

tornadoes, 74
triacyl glycerol, 39
triple bonds, 22

U
United Nations, Kyoto Protocol
    and, 73
unsaturated fats, 39
uracil, 40–41
urea, 2

V
volcanoes, atmosphere and, 59–60

W
water, 44, 46
weather, 62, 74
weathering, 45, 52
welding, 29
wind power, 83
Wohler, Friedrich, 2

ABOUT THE AUTHOR

Frankly, organic chemistry has never been a favorite topic for free-lance science writer **KRISTA WEST**. It's hard. But in order to study her first passion—biology—Krista had to learn some serious chemistry. Once she understood that the behavior of parts inside the atom helps determine the behavior of larger things like lions and leaves, she was hooked. Krista writes chemistry, biology, and Earth science books for young adults from her home in Fairbanks, Alaska. She holds a B.S. in zoology from the University of Washington and masters degrees in earth science and journalism from Columbia University.